# Bibliology

BUILDING CONVICTION AND CONFIDENCE IN THE BIBLE

REGULAR BAPTIST PRESS
3715 N. Ventura Drive
Arlington Heights, IL 60004-7678

## The Doctrinal Basis of Our Curriculum

A more detailed statement with references is available upon request.

- The verbal, plenary inspiration of the Scriptures
- Only one true God
- The Trinity of the Godhead
- The Holy Spirit and His ministry
- The personality of Satan
- The Genesis account of creation
- Original sin and the fall of man
- The virgin birth of Christ
- Salvation through faith in the shed blood of Christ
- The bodily resurrection and priesthood of Christ
- Grace and the new birth
- Justification by faith
- Sanctification of the believer
- The security of the believer
- The church
- The ordinances of the local church: baptism by immersion and the Lord's Supper
- Biblical separation—ecclesiastical and personal
- Obedience to civil government
- The place of Israel
- The pretribulation rapture of the church
- The premillennial return of Christ
- The millennial reign of Christ
- Eternal glory in Heaven for the righteous
- Eternal torment in Hell for the wicked

Alex Bauman, Editor

Bibliology: Building Conviction and Confidence in the Bible
Adult Bible Study Student Book
Vol. 64 • No. 5

www.regularbaptistpress.org • 1-800-727-4440
Printed in U.S.A.

RBP0157 • ISBN: 978-1-62940-227-7

# Contents

# Preface

Bibliology is the study of the Bible. It is different than Bible study. Bible study involves examining a passage to ascertain its meaning so that it might be properly interpreted and applied to one's life. Bibliology answers foundational questions about the Bible: What is the Bible? How did it come to be? Is it trustworthy? And what is the Bible about? This Bibliology course will answer those foundational questions so that we might develop convictions about the Bible's trustworthiness and grow in our confidence in the Bible. Being confident in the Bible is important to realizing its transformational effects on our lives.

Furthermore, this course addresses some of the attacks on the truthfulness and reliability of the Bible. The Bible has historically always been under attack. Recently the most serious attacks are coming from inside Evangelicalism. This course provides answers to those attacks that will reassure you that God's Word is indeed reliable and accurate.

Keep in mind that this course is more than an academic exercise. It is also intended to be an encouragement to be confident in what the Bible says, to develop convictions from the Word, and then live in accordance with those convictions.

# God's Revelation

## Scripture Focus

Ps. 19:1–11; Rom. 1:18–20; Heb. 1:1–4; 2 Tim. 3:16, 17

## Theme

God has revealed His truth to humanity.

### Memory Verses

*"The heavens declare the glory of God; and the firmament sheweth his handiwork. . . . The law of the Lord is perfect, converting the soul: the testimony of the Lord is sure, making wise the simple" (Psalm 19:1, 7).*

## GETTING STARTED

The Bible is essentially God's message to humanity about His character and ways. But it is not the only message He has given to us. He has provided us with other means of revelation. It is important to see how God's revelation in the Scriptures fits into His overall plan to reveal Himself to humanity. It is also important to understand the purpose of His revelation. So this lesson presents God's overall plan to reveal Himself and thereby lays a foundation for building convictions about and confidence in the Bible, God's most informative revelation of Himself.

1. Describe your level of confidence in the Bible.

2. How has your level of confidence in the Bible affected the Bible's influence on your life?

God has supplied revelation for all of humanity. He offers information we desperately need. There is no higher priority in life than establishing an eternal relationship with God. He Himself has taken the initiative to be sure we have what we need.

## Revelation Comes from God

Revelation is the work of God by which He makes Himself and His purposes known to mankind. This definition does not specify the means by which God sends revelation, because the means are secondary to His purpose in giving it. His purpose is to allow us to have knowledge of Him.

Revelation existed before Adam sinned. Of course, the heavens declared the glory of God from the moment of their creation. But even in the Garden of Eden, Adam and Eve needed God to show them truth. Neither of them knew their purpose as individuals or as a couple until God taught them. On the sixth day of creation, God first showed Adam what he needed to know: Adam was incomplete without a helper suited to him. After that, God created Eve and brought her to Adam (Gen. 2:18–24). Man's exulting poem, *This is now bone of my bones, and flesh of my flesh*, shows his response to God. God initiated revelation to man, showed his need to him, and then revealed that He had met the need.

Because sin has permeated our world, we have an even more urgent need of revelation from God. *As it is written, There is none righteous, no, not one* (Rom. 3:10). Sin alienates people from God and creates a need they try to fill with idol worship.

3. Read Psalm 115:1–8. Contrast what the passage says about God with what it says about idols.

Idol worship reveals that humanity's universal need is to commune with God. But since sin warps their thinking process (Rom. 1:28), they cannot think their way out of the mess of sin. In fact, their understanding is darkened (Eph. 4:18), and their minds are hostile and rebellious against God. They cannot please Him (Rom. 8:7, 8). Their sinfulness has created a world of error and confusion, and they cannot find the way to peace and life.

But there is grace in God's revelation! When we were blinded by sin, God caused the light of the gospel to shine so we could have light to see (2 Cor. 4:4). At the root of the term translated as *revelation* is the idea of *unveiling*. God unveils what we could not have known on our own but what we needed to live as His child.

4. Was your salvation experience like walking from darkness to light? Explain.

The revelation of God gives us the opportunity to know the will of God. We learn of His nature and of His plan. However, we should realize that God has not revealed everything that He might have revealed.

5. Read Deuteronomy 29:29. To Whom do the secret things belong? To whom do the revealed things belong?

Though God did not reveal all things to humanity, His revelation gives us all we need to know in order to be rightly related to Him.

All revelation, though revealed in different ways, points toward God. We must acknowledge that God's revelation gives us the only opportunity is to know Him and be reconciled to Him. We must also submit to God's revelation rather than being obsessed with what He has not chosen to tell us.

6. What are some truths that God has not revealed to us?

## General Revelation

Some theologians call *general* revelation *natural* revelation. It may be defined as God's work of revealing truth about Himself through the universe

He has created. The first chapters of the Bible reveal God's creative activity. When there was no one else, He existed. When there was nothing, He created something. According to Exodus 20:11, *For in six days the Lord made heaven and earth, the sea, and all that in them is, and rested the seventh day*. Many places in the Bible pick up on this theme, but Romans 1 and Psalm 19 clearly teach the benefits of general revelation.

According to the apostle Paul, judgment hangs over the human race because humans are ignoring the obvious: a creation necessarily points to a Creator. The creation is God's teaching device. It has been announcing God's presence from the day God created it.

7. Read Romans 1:18–20. According to verse 20, what about God can be clearly seen through creation?

8. When have you seen magnificent nature and had their thoughts turn toward God?

Paul asserted that God's creation gives a clear, unmistakable message. Humanity's problem is not that they cannot see what is clear but that they choose to ignore it.

9. According to Romans 1:18, what do people naturally do with the truth they learn about God from nature?

10. How is this reaction played out in society today?

While the creation provides a great benefit for the world—they have evidence of God's existence—they ignore that revelation to their eternal peril.

Paul's thoughts in Romans 1:18–20 might have been sparked by Psalm 19:1–6. Both the heavens and the skies speak volumes about God. They teach day and night (19:2).

11. Read Psalm 19:1–6. Why is it significant that general revelation reaches around the globe?

The heavens and the skies teach across the cultural barriers of the globe (Ps. 19:3, 4). As an example, God offers the daily journey of the sun. Just as the sun illumines everything on the face of the earth, so the universe illumines the God Who created it.

God's character is glorious (Ps. 19:1). The word *glory* contains the concept of *worthiness*, of *value that is unmistakable*. God has done that which no one else can do. Not only did He create something out of nothing, but He also made it vast and grand and complex. The general revelation of creation shows us a God Who is worthy of worship.

However, general revelation is limited in its effect. It shows, but it does not speak. We learn of God's existence, power, and glory. But we learn relatively little of His character. General revelation does not reveal the way to a relationship with God, that is, the way of salvation.

12. Read Romans 8:18–22. How does the curse on the universe affect the effectiveness of general revelation?

The majesty of creation should draw us to the Creator. We should become curious, asking how we could know the One Who has the ability to create a system as large as the universe. To find the answer, we need special revelation.

## Special Revelation

Special revelation is not *special* because it is better in quality than *general* revelation. Its uniqueness lies in its narrower purpose. In special revelation, God revealed truth that will bring mankind into a saving relationship with

Him and will meet their needs within that relationship. In a sense, special revelation is built on the foundation of general revelation. Those who respond to the creation's call to learn of the Creator must do so on His terms.

## Prophets

God used an interesting variety of methods to provide special revelation. The prophet served as the *mouth* of the Lord. Prophets never gave their own ideas as if they were the originators of God's message. The Spirit carried them along as they provided revelation (2 Pet. 1:21). We know very little about the way God revealed His message to the prophets. When *the word of the Lord* came to the prophet, he relayed the same words to the people. What he received, he gave, so God must have spoken with the prophets in their own languages.

13. Read Deuteronomy 13:1–5. What do God's instructions to Israel about false prophets tell you about how seriously God took the role of prophets?

The prophets were careful to state the divine authority for their messages, so the announcement *thus saith the Lord* rings throughout the Old Testament. Failure to heed the prophet was failure to heed God (1 Sam. 15:1–3, 19–23).

## Miracles

God also used miracles as a form of special revelation. When God created the universe, He designed its mechanisms. The universe operates by the laws that God placed into effect. Since He is the creator of both the universe and its systems, He may choose to bypass His laws to convey a message.

14. What are some Biblical examples of God superseding the laws of nature in order to convey a message?

15. Read Exodus 7:5. What message did God send to the Egyptians by bringing the plagues upon them?

As God intensified the plagues on Egypt (Exod. 7—12), He made it clear that Pharaoh could not seek a natural explanation for the miracles. The plague of flies did not affect Goshen, the homeland of Israel, though the flies made life unbearable for the Egyptians (8:20–24). This special revelation was designed *to the end [that] thou mayest know that I am the Lord in the midst of the earth* (8:22).

In addition to this evangelistic purpose, the Lord's miracles affected His people, drawing them to a deeper knowledge of His love and care for them. During Israel's forty years of wandering in the wilderness, God brought miraculous food daily in the form of manna. He provided water out of a rock where there was no water. The Israelites' shoes and clothing did not wear out as the people traveled. His miracles tested and humbled Israel so the people would depend on Him and His Word alone. All of this proved that God cared enough for His people to discipline them and draw them back to Himself (Deut. 8:1–5).

## Visions and Dreams

On occasion, God used visions and dreams as special revelation. He supplied the interpretation of these revelations, lest the recipient choose the wrong option from the many possible interpretations. Joseph's rise to prominence was revealed in advance by his dreams (Gen. 37). Later God gave Pharaoh dreams that made sense only when He revealed the interpretation through Joseph (Gen. 41). Much later, Ezekiel had a vision of the temple that God will command Israel to rebuild during the millennial rule of the Lord Jesus Christ. The reality of the vision and the certainty of its fulfillment are seen in the precise design and dimensions revealed (Ezek. 40—43). God no longer uses visions and dreams to convey His messages because the Bible is God's complete revelation for today.

Special revelation is forever tangible and observable in the person of Jesus Christ and in the record of God's Word, the Bible. All the means of special revelation pale when compared to the revelation of Jesus Christ and the Bible.

## The Lord Jesus Christ

As God in flesh, Jesus is the absolutely perfect revelation of God. John 1:1 and 2 plainly teach the eternality of Christ. As the Word, He has always existed and has always been God.

16. Read John 1:1, 2, and 14. Whose glory do we see when we observe the life of Christ?

Hebrews 1:1–4 makes clear that Jesus is the absolutely perfect revelation of God. We learn about God's glory and person from the life of Christ.

17. Read John 14:7–11. What did Christ convey to His disciples about His relationship with the Father?

Our Lord Jesus not only showed us the person of God the Father but also the way to God the Father. He *purged our sins* by His death on the cross (Heb. 1:3). Special revelation goes far beyond stretching our minds with information that we would never have guessed from general revelation. It draws us to the knowledge of God. It gives us an opportunity to be rightly related to God.

## The Word of God

We know about special revelation because God recorded some of it in the Bible (2 Tim. 3:16, 17). But the Bible is far more than a record of God's special revelation. The Bible is special revelation. It is God-breathed; therefore, it is miraculous in essence and accurate in its entirety. As a whole, it is designed to reveal God to us and draw us to a vital relationship with Him. God's Word has extraordinary value because it leads us to Him (Ps. 19:7–11). During the succeeding lessons of this course, we will explore the unique aspects of the Bible's special revelation.

18. Why might we sometimes take God's Word for granted and fail to treat it as the very Word of God?

Special revelation gives us the opportunity to know God. That knowledge leads to a growing relationship with Him. We need to learn a great deal, but the task is not unpleasant. The Lord saw our need for Him and responded with just the sort of revelation we needed to gain true knowledge. Psalm 19:7–11 teaches that the Word is absolutely trustworthy and that it will bring change to our lives. When we immerse ourselves in God's Word, we begin to know the Lord as we desire. His Word will not disappoint us.

## MAKING IT PERSONAL

You probably would agree intellectually that the Bible is a part of God's special revelation to humanity. Perhaps you would even be willing to go to battle to defend the Bible. But does your day-to-day treatment of the Bible reveal that you believe the Bible is revelation from God?

19. What would characterize a person's if he truly believed the Bible is part of God's special revelation to humanity?

20. What would a stranger conclude about the Bible's value by watching your life for a week?

Belief that the Scriptures are part of God's revelation to you should lead you to be hungry for the Scriptures and to desire to what to know and understand them.

21. How has a fresh look at the Bible as God's special revelation to you affected your desire to know and understand God's Word?

Once we get a taste of the power of God's Word, we delight in it and want to know it better. The problem is often that we don't know God's Word and are mostly unacquainted with its life-changing effects. Let this course on Bibliology encourage you to be diligent in Bible study.

# Inspiration of Scripture

## Scripture Focus

Matt. 5:18; 2 Tim. 3:16, 17; 1 Pet. 1:25; 2 Pet. 1:2–4, 20, 21

## Theme

God Himself is the source of every word of Scripture.

**Memory Verse**

*"Verily I say unto you, Till heaven and earth pass, one jot or one tittle shall in no wise pass from the law, till all be fulfilled" (Matthew 5:18).*

## GETTING STARTED

Memes have flooded the Internet with sarcastic, funny, and sometimes inspirational messages. But most of the time the messages are just plain dumb. Unfortunately, the memes also tend to stick in our minds. We can't help but share them when the topic of *favorite memes* comes up in a conversation.

1. Do you tend to remember the dumb sayings or the inspirational ones?

2. How have inspirational sayings affected your life?

Unfortunately, some people read the Bible as if it were a book of inspirational memes. It is far more, for the Bible is God's inspired Word. It is more than inspirational; it is powerfully transformational. This study will cover the topic of the *inspiration* of Scripture and the Bible's subsequent trustworthiness.

## SEARCHING THE SCRIPTURES

### Definition of Inspiration

The Greek word *theopneustos*, translated *inspiration*, literally means *Godbreathed*. If you have ever said, *Don't breathe a word about this!* then you understand the relationship between the breath and the word. The English word *inspiration* comes to us from the Latin word *inspirare*, which means *to breathe in*. The Latin word is used as the translation of the Greek word in the old Latin Bible (the Vulgate) in 2 Timothy 3:16 and 17 and 2 Peter 1:21, two key passages that support the doctrine of inspiration.

When we speak of the doctrine of inspiration, we mean that the Scriptures came directly from God. He breathed them out. He is the source of the words.

*Inspiration* may be defined as *God's superintendence of human authors so that, using their own individual personalities, they composed and recorded without error His revelation to man in the words of the original autographs* (Charles Ryrie, *A Survey of Bible Doctrine* [Chicago: Moody Publishers, 1972], 38).

### The Scriptures Are God-breathed

*Who told you to do that?* is a question that seeks an authority to justify behavior. If the questioner respects the authority that authorized the action, then the one being questioned is absolved. The inspiration of the Scriptures places the Bible's authority with its author: God.

3. Read 2 Timothy 3:16, 17; 2 Peter 1:20, 21. What do you learn from these passages about what Scripture is not?

4. What do you learn from these passages about what Scripture is?

Since God authored the Bible, we should expect it to reflect His perfect character and therefore be free from error. The Bible is not the product of human ingenuity or abilities. If it were, man's ideas would taint it and cause it to be self-contradictory. The Bible came from the mouth of God. Over two thousand times in the Old Testament, the prophets attest, *Thus saith the Lord*. The Scriptures are God's own words of truth. The writings reflect the authority of His words.

## The Scriptures Had Human Writers

You need to read only one of Paul's letters and the book of James to understand that the writers' styles are reflected in their writings. Yet both letters are equally inspired by God and designed to help us become like our Savior.

5. How does the fact that human writers put their personalities into the Scriptures affect your trust in the Bible's accuracy?

6. Who gave writers like Paul and James their personalities?

7. How does knowing God gave specific personalities to human writers help you trust the Bible?

Recognizing writers' personalities within Scripture does not diminish the divine nature of God's Word. The Holy Spirit was still the source of God's Word. The presence of the writers' personalities in the inspired Word is a testament to God's sovereignty. He gave the writers the personalities that would reflect exactly the style of writing God wanted in the parts of Scripture that they wrote.

Peter laid a foundation for truth: *No prophecy of the scripture is of any private interpretation* (2 Pet. 1:20, 21). The Bible is not merely a compilation of the teachings of wise men who collaborated to produce a literary work. The Scriptures are not merely the result of *the will of man*.

The Holy Spirit arranged for the writing of the Word. He did this as He *moved* the writers of the Word. The word *moved* in verse 21 is not a precise literary term. The other New Testament use of the term occurs in Acts 27:15, which tells about Paul's ship being driven along by the wind of a storm. The wind determined the direction and destination of the ship. However, the passengers could still move around within the ship, moving between decks and cabins. This occurrence may illustrate the way the Spirit used the personalities of the individual writers of Scripture. Their writing styles differed, yet the outcome was the inspired Word of God.

## The Scriptures Are God's Word to Humanity

The Bible is essentially a relational book, not a book of abstract ideas. God used writing to bring His relational message to the human race He created. There are many questions the Bible does not address; it is not an encyclopedia. God never intended to use the Bible to answer all of mankind's questions.

8. What questions does the Bible not address?

9. How do the subjects addressed in the Bible point to what is really important in life?

The Bible addresses people's greatest needs. We cannot rightfully wish for more instruction or long for more direction from God. He has already told us all we need to know.

10. Read 2 Peter 1:2–4. How does God's Word fit into the picture of having all things that pertain to life and godliness?

All we need to live a life pleasing to God is found in God's Word. It even tells us what we are to do when we don't understand how to live it out. According to James 1:5, God will grant our requests for wisdom. God's inspired Word is our way to know God.

## The Original Manuscripts Are Inspired

Inspiration applies to the autographs of the Bible. The term *autographs* refers to the original manuscripts. For instance, the letter to the Romans, which Tertius penned as Paul dictated to him, was the autograph of Romans (Rom. 16:22). In reference to Paul's own writings, Paul asserted that what he wrote was from the Spirit and thus inspired. He wrote, *Which things also we speak, not in the words which man's wisdom teacheth, but which the Holy Ghost teacheth; comparing spiritual things with spiritual* (1 Cor. 2:13). None of the autographs survived.

Inspiration does not pertain to copies of the autographs. However, that is not a problem. We can trust our Bibles because God has promised to preserve His Word (1 Pet. 1:25). Considering our Lord's words in Matthew 5:18, we should expect God to do exactly that: *Verily I say unto you, Till heaven and earth pass, one jot or one tittle shall in no wise pass from the law, till all be fulfilled.* The Lord Jesus didn't say how God would preserve His Word. Yet looking back on the last two thousand years, we find some amazing methods.

We have grown so accustomed to having printed books, copy machines, and computers that we should pause to remember that they are relatively recent inventions. In the days before the printing press, any copy of a literary work was a hand copy, or manuscript. The Masoretes were Jewish copyists who exemplified the care that was used in hand-copying the Word of God. They counted letters and words to be sure that the copied document matched the original exactly.

Was this process effective? Judge by this: until the 1950s, the *oldest* Hebrew Old Testament available to us was a copy from around AD 900. Since Malachi was written around 400 BC, our best copy was over 1,300 years old. The discovery of the Dead Sea Scrolls provided us with Hebrew manuscripts that dated to the second century BC. These manuscripts, over one thousand years older than the ones already available to us, contained virtually no major differences from the ones we had. All variances were minor and understandable, considering the human element of copying copious letters and words.

The New Testament manuscripts show similar accuracy. Thousands of copies of all or part of the New Testament are available to us. These include very old papyrus segments and fairly well-preserved vellum (animal skin) copies. A fragment of the Gospel of John was found in Egypt, dated to around AD 125. Since John probably wrote his works late in his life, in as little as thirty years after their writing, his Gospel found its way to Egypt. Complete New Testament manuscripts can be dated to the fourth century. There are even early translations of the New Testament from the second century.

As scholars compare these many different manuscripts, they find the same situation as with the Old Testament; that is, the New Testament has been marvelously preserved for us. Our God wants us to know His Word, and He has assured that possibility by preserving His Word for us.

There is no need to worry that we have lost something or that God's Word has become corrupted since the days of the originals. In essence, we can speak of our Bible today as being inspired because it is an accurate representation of the inspired originals.

## The Words Are Inspired

The individual words of Scripture are inspired, not just the concepts or ideas that lie behind the words. It would seem almost unnecessary to make this point, given what 2 Timothy 3:16 and 2 Peter 1:21 teach us. After all, concepts can be expressed only through words. God could not impress a concept on the mind of a prophet; He would have to use words to communicate the concept.

Nowhere does the Bible urge believers to know the general ideas of God's revelation or to give attention to the basic ideas that God taught. We are to know the very words of God. The prophet Moses exhorted Israel to heed *the commandments, the statutes, and the judgments, which the Lord your God commanded to teach you* (Deut. 6:1). He insisted that the commandments be on their hearts (6:6). Near the end of Deuteronomy, God is even more pointed about the Israelites' responsibility to heed His specific words.

11. Read Deuteronomy 30:15, 16. How important was it for the Israelites to know the very words of God's commands, statutes, and judgments?

The New Testament motivates us to hold a similar regard for the Bible's specific words. For example, in Galatians 3:16 Paul made a point based on the difference between the singular and plural use of the word *seed* in the Genesis record of God's promises to Abraham (Gen. 13:15;

17:8). God holds us accountable for exactly what He has said.

Even the smallest letter and the least pen stroke of Scripture is inspired (Matt. 5:17, 18). Jesus came to fulfill (or bring to completion) the promises that God made in the Law and the Prophets. *The Law and the Prophets* was an expression the Jews used for the Old Testament. Jesus promised to fulfill all of them, even down to the smallest letter and the least stroke of a pen. In other words, He would fulfill the promises completely and precisely.

The smallest letter, the *yod*, looks somewhat like an English apostrophe. It makes the sound of a *Y*. The smallest part of a letter would be the pen stroke that differentiates similar letters. The bit of ink that makes the difference between a *C* and a *G* in English letters could illustrate this distinction. Our Lord's point for His disciples becomes clear: God inspired even the smallest parts of His Word, and He plans to bring His Word to completion.

## The Whole Text of Scripture Is Inspired

*Plenary inspiration* refers to the inspiration of the whole text of Scripture.

12. Read Genesis 1:1; 10:4; John 3:16, 17; 2 Timothy 4:20. Which of these passages would you deem most important? Why?

13. Which of these passages does not seem important? Why?

14. Read 2 Timothy 3:16, 17. According to these verses, how inspired are each of the passages we read?

No matter how trivial passages may seem, all of them are as inspired as more important passages (2 Tim. 3:16, 17). *Scripture* refers to God's Word. In the times of the New Testament, the term originally applied to the Old Testament. However, God was inspiring more writings. In 1 Timothy 5:18 Paul offered two quotations from Scripture. The first comes from Deuteronomy 25:4, and the second comes from Luke 10:7. Paul recognized Luke's Gospel as Scripture. Even in the early days of the church, the apostles recognized the inspired quality of God's Word given through them. Thus Paul reminded Timothy that there are no degrees of inspiration or parts of the Bible that are anything less than *God-breathed*. The gospel of John is just as inspired as the details and genealogies of Leviticus and Numbers.

Because it is inspired, all of Scripture is worthy of careful study. Based on plenary inspiration, we ought to study the whole of the Word of God. Some portions are easier to understand, as Peter indicated (2 Pet. 3:16). However, all of Scripture has value because God wrote it and designed it for our growth in grace and knowledge of Christ.

The implications of verbal plenary inspiration are vast. We have possession of a book that is God's revelation. We can have confidence that all of it is of divine origin. This should motivate us to study, for we can know God and His will for our lives with certainty.

## MAKING IT PERSONAL

Because of inspiration, we can have confidence that we are trusting in and living by the truth.

15. How have you responded to the trustworthiness of God's Word?

16. How should we respond to the trustworthiness of God's Word?

In a world where bluster can seem more important than substance, knowledge that the Bible is divine authority is a source of both comfort and strength.

17. How has confidence in God's Word helped you during a difficult time?

18. What current circumstances in your life are you better able to face because of your confidence in God's Word?

# Inerrancy and Infallibility

LESSON 3

## Scripture Focus

Ps. 19:7–12; Prov. 21:1; 30:5; Luke 24:13–35; John 17:17; 1 Tim. 1:4; 4:7; 2 Tim. 4:1–5; Titus 1:2; 2 Peter 1:16

## Theme

God's inspiration of the Scriptures ensures that they are inerrant and infallible.

**Memory Verse**

*"Every word of God is pure: he is a shield unto them that put their trust in him" (Proverbs 30:5).*

## GETTING STARTED

Wikipedia is an online encyclopedia that anyone can edit as they see fit. While is it helpful in some regards, some of the articles were no doubt written by people who don't really know the subjects.

1. What might you be comfortable looking up on Wikipedia?

2. What questions would you not go to Wikipedia for answers?

While the founders of Wikipedia succeeded in creating an editable online encyclopedia, they could never promote their site as completely trustworthy. There are some theologians who are trying to pin that same criticism on the Bible, saying it can't be completely trusted. This study addresses that criticism and presents the case for the inerrancy and infallibility of the Bible.

## SEARCHING THE SCRIPTURES

### Inerrancy

The word *inerrancy* comes from the Latin word *errare*, meaning *to wander*. That meaning seems to suggest that *inerrancy* is associated with a departure from something. *Departing* is not a good action to associate with *truth*. But the Latin prefix *in* is negative. So *inerrancy* means to be *free from error*. Whatever is *inerrant* could be said to have *not wandered from the truth*. When we say the Bible is inerrant, we are saying that it is without error. But a fuller definition of *Biblical* inerrancy is needed to understand its full application.

*Biblical inerrancy* means the Bible is free from error and that it speaks the truth whether it addresses doctrine, ethics, or history. Of course the Bible records lies and deception, but it never presents them as truth.

The term *inerrancy* is not found in the Bible. But we do know that the Bible is inspired (2 Tim. 3:16). Inerrancy is the logical outworking of verbal, plenary inspiration.

3. What would you have to conclude about God if the Bible was both inspired and filled with errors and false claims?

4. Read Titus 1:2; John 17:17. What truths about God point to the fact that His Word must be free from error?

Proverbs 30:5 says that *every word of God is pure*. The word *pure* has the idea of being refined and found to be pure. When God's words are *heated up* and *melted down*, not one drop of *impurity* comes to the surface. There is nothing to skim off the top. All God's words are absolutely true, including those recorded in the Bible.

## Infallibility

It was impossible for the writers to record an error of any kind as they penned the Scriptures since they were under the guidance of the Holy Spirit. That impossibility of error is what is meant by the word *infallible.* The Bible is inerrant because it is infallible, and it is infallible because it is inspired. To say the Bible is neither inerrant nor infallible is to flatly deny it is inspired by God.

We should note that during the course of the transmission of Scripture from the originals, minor scribal errors were made in the copies. As a result, there are textual variants in the manuscripts we have today. Studying the manuscripts and comparing them helps us sort out the variations and complete highly accurate texts in their original languages. Such a study also shows that the variations are rather inconsequential, affecting not one foundational doctrine. These textual variations are not proofs against the inerrancy and infallibility of Scripture. The terms *inerrant* and *infallible* apply to the original manuscripts. Since those originals were perfect, we can have the utmost confidence in our Bibles today. The Bible is the Word of God.

## Importance

If the Bible is not inerrant, then there has to be an authority over the Bible to tell us which parts of it are true and which parts are not. The only authority over the Bible is God. So no matter to whom or to what we might appeal to establish what is true in the Bible, we would be consulting a source that is inadequate and unauthoritative. God is the Bible's ultimate authority, and He has spoken quite plainly in His Word about its truthfulness and reliability.

5. Read Psalm 19:12. Why is every human unqualified to stand as a judge over the Bible?

The inerrancy of Scripture gives us confidence as we interpret it. We know that it is true and therefore its meaning and subsequent application will affect our lives (Ps. 19:7–11). Reading the Bible with doubt about its veracity robs the believer of the Bible's benefits. Inerrancy is vital to sustained spiritual growth in a believer (John 17:17).

## Arguments Based on Language

It is important for us to understand some of the arguments for doubting the Bible's inerrancy so we are prepared to answer them and don't fall prey to them.

Some theologians argue that the Bible cannot be inerrant because it contains imprecise language. They demand the Bible must be exact in all that it reports and describes in order for it to be unqualifiedly inerrant. For example, they would list round numbers, non-scientific descriptions (e.g., saying the sun *rises* and *sets*), symbolic language, and generalizations (e.g., using *all* instead of *almost all*) as qualifications to inerrancy of Scripture. But Biblical inerrancy does not demand that the Bible be as precise and accurate as possible in all that it reports and claims. We all use imprecise language as part of our normal speech. Such language is not considered a lie in any context. Saying the sun rose in the morning is accurate in that the sun appears from an earthly perspective to rise and travel across the sky. Inerrancy allows for imprecision and generalization. When the Bible doesn't *claim* to be precise, we should accept the imprecision or generalization as part of God's inerrant Word.

6. Read Matthew 14:13–21. List five details that this account does not include.

7. What would the Bible be like if it had to be as accurate and precise as possible in every single subject it touched and event it recorded?

The Bible doesn't set a standard for itself that demands absolute preciseness in everything it reports. But it does use precise language when it communicates precise doctrines. For example, doctrines such as the holiness of God (Isa. 6:3; Rev. 4:8), the way of salvation (John 11:25, 26), and the deity of Christ (John 1:1, 2) are readily apparent in the Bible.

## Arguments Based on Content

Ancient near eastern cultures wrote stories about nature, humanity, and deities. Modern scholars call these stories *myths* and generally regard them as fictional. Some of these myths seem to have similarities with accounts in the Pentateuch. Based on these similarities, some evangelical theologians conclude that the Bible's account of creation and other events must either be based on or borrowed from the myths. Those theologians don't go so far as to deny the Bible is inerrant, but they do qualify their definition of inerrancy. They argue that the Pentateuch was based on the cultural understanding of history at that time. Since the cultures around the unidentified *writers* of the Pentateuch believed in the myths about origins, the believe the writers incorporated those stories into the Pentateuch naively. The writers thought they were writing in accordance with actual accounts when in fact they were basing their writings on fictional myths. The theologians who hold to this view of inerrancy believe that God, knowing full well that the stories were myths, overrode the human writers' ineptness and immature understanding to communicate His divine purpose through the myths. The theologians conclude that the result is a conglomeration of stories that are the product of both human myths and divine inspiration. The scholars say that the divine purpose that God infused into the myths was to teach the children of Israel that they were to worship Him alone. So even though the Biblical text was based on made up stories, God sovereignly preserved His theological intent in the Pentateuch. The Pentateuch, the theologians say, has value today because of what it communicates about theology rather than what it says about history. The theologians who deny the historicity of the Pentateuch believe that later in Israel's history the methods of keeping track of actual historical events matured so that the monarchial history of Israel does indeed reflect historical events rather than myths.

The proponents of the qualified view of inerrancy point to Christ as an example of a mix of perfect deity and imperfect humanity. They say that Christ's human side was limited, meaning He didn't necessarily excel at things such as math or carpentry. Also they suggest that the simple fact that Christ had a human body meant He must have been physically less than perfect. His humanity had flaws that limited Him and caused Him to make mistakes. Yet He was perfectly God and completely holy. The proponents of the qualified inerrancy compare Christ's mix of flawed humanity and perfect deity to Scriptures. Since the Bible was written by sinful humans, it inherently has evidence of human flaws. But since the Bible was also inspired by God, we can consider it inerrant. The proponents of a qualified inerrancy use this analogy to make room for the inclusions of *myths* and other supposed *imperfections* in the Bible. According to them, the Bible is inerrant in that it fulfills God's purpose. It is God's theological purposes then that should be the theologian's focus. And, according to those who qualify the inerrancy of Scripture, determining which parts of the Bible were subjected to human limits and understanding is an exercise for the scholar.

## Answers to Qualified Inerrancy Advocates

A qualified inerrancy is obviously quite different than a Biblical view of inerrancy. The redefinition of inerrancy and selective qualifications of certain Scriptures as myths or mistakes, while intended to answer questions and build faith, actually do little to bolster one's confidence in the Bible. For how could anyone be absolutely sure that what he was reading was actually true? And how might he know for certain that he was indeed smart enough to be able to ascertain God's theological points from the stories he supposed were myths?

So how do we answer this seemingly intellectual attack on inerrancy from inside evangelicalism? First, we must trust what the Bible says about itself. No one can speak as authoritatively as the Bible's own record because the Scriptures are God's very words. The Bible is actually very clear that it is not based on myth and that myths (fables) are not a reliable source for truth.

8. Read 2 Peter 1:16. What did Peter say about the Biblical accounts of the power and coming of the Lord Jesus Christ?

9. Read 2 Timothy 4:1–5. What did the apostle Paul instruct pastors concerning the Word of God and fables?

Paul taught pastor Timothy to reject any sources that people wanted to add to the Bible as authoritative (1 Tim. 1:4; 4:7). If the books of the Pentateuch are merely myths with a theological message, then Paul would have been telling Timothy to reject the Pentateuch.

Second, we must recognize the integral part history plays in God's revelation of Himself. The historical record is an essential part of Scripture; it is the vehicle through which God reveals truth about Himself and His relationship with humanity. We cannot know God as He intends if we relegate the Bible's history to fictional myths collected because of human naivety. makes a strong case for seeing the Bible's historical records as essential to understanding the message of the Bible.

10. Read Luke 24:13–27. For what did Jesus use the history found in the Old Testament?

11. Read Luke 24:28–35. What was the result?

Third, a true definition of *myth* shows that the Old Testament could in no way be myth or even be based on myths of other cultures. John N. Oswalt, author of *The Bible among the Myth* (2009, Zondervan), carefully defined myths by demonstrating that ancient myths were born out of the belief that all things are continuous, meaning nature, humans, and the divine all share a real oneness. That means both nature and divine have human qualities that can be reflected by the characters in the myths. The myths, then, are expressions of the continuities of the human, natural, and divine realms. For the ancient pagan societies, the myths became the means of bringing the order of the ideal divine realm into the chaotic human realm to give it stability and victory over chaos. For all humans realize that though nature has cycles and some stability, it can also be chaotic and randomly destructive. When the ancient myths about the ideal are retold, the positive, desirable results of those stories are brought into the chaotic now so that the ideal might be realized.

When the worldview behind the ancient pagan myths is considered, the idea that the Bible was written based on those myths becomes absurd. Are these pagan myths the best God could do in conveying Scripture? Was He at the mercy of the limitations of naïve human writers? Most certainly not.

12. Read Job 42:1, 2; Psalm 115:3; Proverbs 21:1. What limits are there on what God can do?

So, why would anyone try to redefine inerrancy? Why go through such pains to prove the Bible is not all that conservative fundamentalists believe it is?

## Ambitions of Qualified Inerrancy Advocates

For as long as God's Word has been known, there have been those who have tried to discredit it, redefine it, or outright deny it. Starting with Satan in the Garden of Eden and ending with Satan (Gen. 3:1–5) near the end of the millennial Kingdom of Christ (Rev. 20:7–10), the attack on God's Word has never ceased and will continue until it is all fulfilled. We shouldn't be surprised when some from within evangelicalism also attack God's Word. The sin nature wants to discredit what God says is true. It wants to at the very least limit God in some way. For a limited God appears to be less authoritative. And when people limit God, they grab some of His authority for themselves. If God's Word is not fully inerrant, then they believe they have the right to define its limits.

God's Word demands that people approach it humbly and submissively. There is no place for pride when it comes to understanding the Bible.

13. Read James 4:6. What is God's response to those who approach Him with pride?

Pride prohibits people from truly understanding God's Word. It drives them to remold it and shape it in ways that make them appear intellectually superior to others. Humility takes God at His word.

## MAKING IT PERSONAL

14. How has your perspective on the importance of inerrancy changed as a result of this lesson?

15. Write out a statement describing your beliefs concerning the inerrancy of Scripture.

16. Write out a statement of submission to the authority of Scripture.

17. What will submission to the authority of Scripture look like in your life?

# Canonicity of Scripture

LESSON 4

## Scripture Focus

Luke 11:51; Acts 17:11, 12; Gal. 1:6, 7, 11, 12; 1 Thess. 2:13; Heb. 4:12; 2 Pet. 1:21

## Theme

God made it obvious which books were inspired Scriptures and therefore were canonical.

### Memory Verses

*"But I certify you, brethren, that the gospel which was preached of me is not after man. For I neither received it of man, neither was I taught it, but by the revelation of Jesus Christ"*
*(Galatians 1:11, 12).*

## GETTING STARTED

Imagine working for a contractor who tried to save money by not purchasing measuring tapes, asking you to estimate your measurements instead. Talk about a disaster. Nothing can be properly built without some way of consistent, accurate measuring. There must be a standard.

1. How well would you trust your ability to guess lengths?

2. Name some situations in which you would want an exact measurement instead of a guess.

The sixty-six books that make up the Bible all had to measure up before being accepted as Scripture. The measuring stick was strict and consistent. This study is about the standard by which each of the books was judged.

## SEARCHING THE SCRIPTURES

### Definition of Canonicity

The word *canon* comes from the Latin word, meaning *ruler, rule, model, standard*. The Romans borrowed this word from the Greek language (*kanon, kanna*), in which it meant a reed that was used as a measuring rod. In that sense a yardstick could be called a canon. In time, the word *canon* came to be used for items that had been measured and found to meet the standard.

In the earliest years of the Christian faith, believers recognized that certain books were *inspired* by God, or *breathed out* by Him, when they were written. These were recognized as the *canon* of Scripture.

God determined which writings were to be included in the Canon. The Holy Spirit led the people of Israel and then the people of the early church to recognize which writings were inspired and were to be identified as Scriptures. Five basic principles guided the early Christians in recognizing which books were given by God.

### Test 1: Authority

The early Christians noticed whether a book expressed the authority of God.

3. Read Genesis 15:1; 2 Samuel 7:4; Jeremiah 1:4. What common phrase is found in these verses?

Phrases that attribute words to the Lord clearly state that the words are not simply a man's idea or philosophy. Such statements are found at least 3,808 times in the Old Testament. In other words, God was careful to communicate that the Scriptures are authoritative.

In some of his epistles, the apostle Paul spoke of the authority of his writing.

4. Read 1 Corinthians 11:23. What did Paul say about what he wrote?

5. Read Galatians 1:11, 12. What important doctrine did Paul say he received directly from God?

Paul recognized that nothing he said of his own authority would have been anything more than man's words. He even said that if he or anyone else tried to come up with his own gospel, then that person should be *accursed*, or *eternally condemned* (Gal. 1:8, 9). He fully understood that God was the sole authority for his epistles to the churches.

All the Gospels contain quotations of Jesus Christ and accounts of God speaking from Heaven as well (e.g., Matthew 3:13–17). Many non-Biblical books written over the years of Old and New Testament history did not have the authoritative ring of *thus saith the Lord*.

## Test 2: Writer

Second Peter 1:21 says that God spoke through *holy men* in communicating the Scriptures. In recognizing which books were from God, the early Christians considered the writers of their books (Heb. 1:1). Were the Old Testament writers acknowledged as prophets, lawgivers, or leaders in Israel? Were the New Testament writers recognized as apostles or those who were backed by an apostle? Once the human writers were recognized as authorized by God, the early Christians needed to consider whether each book was written by the name it bears. For those books that don't list an author, they considered whether the book was written by the person traditionally recognized as the author. And for books that are not associated with an author directly or traditionally, they considered whether the book was written in the time period traditionally associated with the book.

A careful examination of all sixty-six books of the Bible shows that every one of them is genuine. Space doesn't allow us to delve into the genuineness test of every Bible book. So this lesson will focus on the genuineness of the Pentateuch, which has come under recent attack from within evangelicalism.

All five books of the Pentateuch have always been traditionally assigned to Moses. The evidence for his authorship is substantial.

6. Read Exodus 17:14. What did God ask Moses to do?

7. Read Exodus 34:27. What did God want Moses to write about in this verse?

Moses not only wrote about what God told him to write, but he also wrote that God told him to write about it. That gives us confidence that God intended for the history of His interaction with Israel to be recorded and that He intended for Moses to be the one to record that history.

Other places in the Penteteuch say that Moses recorded both the Lord's instructions to Israel (Exod. 24:4; Deut. 31:9, 24) and the records of their journeys with the Lord (Num. 33:2). Within the Pentateuch, Moses' writings are referred to as *the words of this law* and *the book of this law* (Deut. 28:58, 61). Outside the Pentateuch Joshua refers to them as *the book of the law of Moses* (Josh. 8:31) while Nehemiah calls the Pentateuch *the book of Moses* (Neh. 13:1). First Kings, 2 Kings, 2 Chronicles, and Daniel also attribute the Pentateuch to Moses.

As shown in the previous lesson, some evangelical theologians believe the Pentateuch was naively based on myths, meaning the stories it contains are not actual historical events. Those same theologians believe Moses didn't write the books. So they would have to agree that a spurious writer made up God's commands to Moses to record historical events (Exod. 17:14; 34:27). For those theologians to claim that the Pentateuch should still be considered inspired is ludicrous. The evidence is clear that Moses wrote the Pentateuch and that he recorded real history under the direction of the Holy Spirit.

8. How important it is for you to know that the words the Pentateuch attributes to God were actually said by God and recorded by Moses?

The New Testament gives further evidence to the fact that Moses wrote the Pentateuch. Luke wrote that after Jesus rose from the dead He explained the Scriptures to the men on the road to Emmaus. Luke said Jesus began at *Moses* (Luke 24:27), a reference to the Pentateuch. The only reason Luke would call the Pentateuch *Moses* is if Moses had actually written the books (cf. Acts 15:21). Paul also called the Pentateuch *Moses* (2 Cor. 3:15).

We must be careful not to let theologians talk us into doubting the genuineness of God's Word, as if they have more authority on the authors of the Scriptures than the Bible has itself.

9. Read Galatians 1:6, 7. What warning did Paul give to the believers in Galatia who had begun to follow a false gospel?

10. Read 1 John 4:1–6. What admonition did John give to believers?

## Test 3: Authenticity

The question of authenticity deals with the content of Scripture. What does it say about God? Is its message consistent with the rest of the Bible? If a book contradicted other Scripture, then it would be suspect. The Bereans set an example by comparing Paul's message to existing Scripture to see whether what he said was in accord with other parts of the Word of God (Acts 17:11).

11. Read Acts 17:12. What was the result of the Berean's faithful testing of the genuineness of Paul's teaching?

Jesus used the Old Testament while He was on earth, and He did so with approval of the text. The Scriptures Jesus used were organized differently than our Old Testaments today. In His Scriptures, Genesis was first and Chronicles was last. While speaking against some lawyers, he mentioned two murdered prophets (Luke 11:51). The first was Abel, whose murder is readily recognized as being in Genesis 4.

12. Read Luke 11:51; 2 Chronicles 24:20, 21. What other murder did Jesus mention?

Jesus spoke to the authority of the entire Old Testament by referring to historical events in the first book, Genesis, and in the last book, Chronicles. He essentially gave His stamp of approval on the first and last books and everything in between. We could say that Jesus used the Old Testament with such confidence that He regarded its historical records as adequate evidence to condemn the religious leaders of His day.

The testimony of all of Scripture is that is in harmonious. There is simply a lack of contradictory doctrines.

## Test 4: Power

The fourth test of canonicity is the evidence that the book was inspired by God. Hebrews 4:12 tells us that the inspired Word of God is *quick, and powerful* and *piercing*. Its message powerfully transforms those who receive it (1 Thess. 2:13). The people of God were able to recognize transforming power in the books that are in the canon of Scripture.

13. Read Hebrews 4:12. What books of the Bible in particular has God used to powerfully affect your life?

14. How do the effects of God's Word help build your confidence in it?

A good way to judge whether a book is inspired is to read it alongside other books that are not part of the Scriptures. The differences between the two become quite evident. For example, books from the Apocrypha, written from about 400 BC to the time of Christ, have a markedly different character than the books included in the canon of Scripture. They do not speak authoritatively; nor are they cohesive with the rest of Scripture.

## Test 5: Reception

The capstone of all questions and tests was if God's people recognized a book in the Bible as being from God when it was written and then continued to do so over the years. The question of what books belonged in the Jewish canon of Scripture had been settled centuries before the time of Christ. The scrolls containing the Law of Moses and the Prophets and the Psalms (Luke 24:44) had been collected in the tabernacle and later in the temple.

15. Read Deuteronomy 31:9–13; Nehemiah 8:1–8. What did Moses command the priests to do?

The early leaders of the church quoted from the Epistles and the Gospels in the same way they quoted from the Old Testament books. Records of worship in the early church indicate that the books of the New Testament were read along with the Old Testament in the second century AD. Formal councils held by the early churches did not announce to the churches which books to use and which to reject. Rather, they offered formal statements that they were using the sixty-six books of the Old and New Testaments because they recognized them to be the Word of God.

The Council of Carthage in AD 397 was the first church council to recognize the twenty-seven books of the New Testament as belonging to the Canon. Though most of the New Testament books had already been considered canonical before then. The books of Hebrews, James, 2 Peter, 2 and 3 John, and Jude were debated some but were eventually recognized. All of the twenty-seven books in the New Testament have proven to be indeed worthy of their place in the canon of Scripture.

The Apocrypha was not accepted by the Jews, nor was it accepted by Christ or others in His time because those books contained historical inaccuracies and strange statements that were morally questionable. Christ never quoted from those books, even though He quoted from almost all the books of the Old Testament. Philo, a Jewish philosopher (20 BC—AD 40), quoted the Old Testament books, but he never included or recognized any of those inter-testamental books as sacred. The Jewish historian Josephus (AD 30–100) explicitly excluded the Apocrypha from the canon of Scripture.

No council of the Christian church gave credibility to the apocryphal books until four hundred years after the time of Christ. The early church actually spoke out against them. It was not until the Council of Trent (1546) that the Roman Catholic church acted to counter the Protestant movement and included the apocryphal books as belonging in the Bible. Just a reading of those books shows that their quality and reliability are not on the same par with inspired Scripture.

## Importance of Canonicity

16. Why is it important for believers to be able to defend the canonicity of Scripture?

Throughout the centuries, various religions have claimed that *extra* books are part of or equal to the sixty-six books of God's Word. As mentioned above, Roman Catholic Bibles contain fourteen additional books between the Old and New Testaments called the Apocrypha.

In 2003, *The Da Vinci Code*, a best-selling novel, alarmed the Christian world by suggesting, among other things, that (1) Jesus and Mary Magdalene were married; (2) Jesus Christ was not the Son of God, but just a *regular* guy; (3) the Bible and the deity of Jesus Christ are hoaxes concocted by Constantine so Christianity would appeal to the pagans under his rule.

By claiming that other Gnostic *books* that taught about Jesus' human traits were purposely left out of the Bible, author Dan Brown gave opportunity for many uncertain readers to further doubt the truth of the Bible. His influence is still reverberating today since being named one of the one hundred most influencing people in the world by Time Magazine in

2005. His novels have been translated into fifty-four different languages and have surpassed the two hundred million mark in sales.

The foundation of God's Word and our faith rests upon the deity of Jesus Christ. Satan will use whatever means possible to cause people to doubt the authenticity of the Bible. Any religion or form of *entertainment* that distorts the Biblical view of Christ or seeks to add to the Word of God offers an unbelieving world even greater reason to question Christianity. Therefore, it is vital that believers hold strongly to the canon of the sixty-six books of the Bible.

## MAKING IT PERSONAL

17. Summarize the canonicity of the Word of God in two or three sentences.

18. Write a personal statement of your confidence that the sixty-six books of the Bible are the complete Word of God.

19. Write out a praise to God that the sixty-six canonical books are known and compiled into the complete Word of God.

20. How might you show your praise to God for assurance concerning the Bible's purity and completeness?

# Transmission of the Bible

## Scripture Focus

Phil. 1:21, 27–30; 2 Tim. 3:16

## Theme

God expects careful attention to accuracy when transmitting Scripture.

### Memory Verse

*"All scripture is given by inspiration of God, and is profitable for doctrine, for reproof, for correction, for instruction in righteousness" (2 Timothy 3:16).*

## GETTING STARTED

The task of Bible translation is just getting started. About two-thirds of the world's seven thousand languages have no Bibles or even portions of Bibles. Getting the Bible in every language seems to be an overwhelming task, but one that would be worth the effort.

1. Do you take for granted having the Bible in English? Explain.

2. What do you know about the sacrifice and effort it took to translate the Bible into English?

This study will focus on the transmission of the Bible to us as well as the need to support Bible translation work today.

## SEARCHING THE SCRIPTURES

God used individuals and groups of people throughout history to transmit the Bible so accurately that we can call our Bibles the *Word of God*. Considering the careful transmission of Scriptural text should build our confidence in our English Bibles.

### Masoretic Text

The Old Testament is based on the Masoretic text, which was transcribed by a group of scribes called Masoretes beginning around the sixth century AD. Their job was completed in the tenth century by scholars at Talmudic academies located in Babylonia and Israel. These Jewish scribes preserved the Scriptures by assembling and codifying every available text at that time. Their goal was to preserve the original text of the Hebrew Old Testament.

The Masoretes' work, as mentioned in lesson 2, was extremely meticulous. They checked that every word and letter was accurate. They also counted the verses, words, and letters in the text, especially noting the middle letter of each page, book, and section so that any revisions or mistakes would stand out in future copies.

The handwritten Masoretic texts we have today date back as far as the late ninth century AD. The oldest printed manuscripts date from the late fifteenth century. When compared, the earliest written and the earliest printed manuscripts are remarkably consistent. As a result, the Masoretic text is considered by scholars to be the authentic Hebrew Bible.

3. Would you say we are fortunate that the Masoretes' work was so careful? Explain.

### Septuagint (LXX)

Around 200 BC Jewish scholars in Alexandria, Egypt, translated the Hebrew Bible into the commonly spoken Greek. This translation was called the *Septuagint*. The name comes from the Latin word for *seventy*, a reference to the seventy-two or so translators that worked on it.

The New Testament, which was written in Greek, often quotes the Septuagint, though not exclusively. Today we have a few early manuscripts of the Septuagint. Among them are the Codex Vaticanus and the Codex Sinaiticus. Those copies are from the fourth century AD. Another manuscript, the Codex Alexandrinus, is from the fifth century. All three manuscripts also include portions of the New Testament in Greek. Some scholars highly value and prioritize these Septuagint manuscripts because they are so early. Yet the manuscripts do show corrections, causing some to question whether their antiquity should give them priority over later and more numerous manuscripts. Overall, the manuscripts are valuable as references for determining the accuracy of the transmission of both the Old and New Testament Scriptures. The parallels between the Masoretic text and the Septuagint are evidence that both are accurate copies of the originals.

In addition to the early versions of the Septuagint, Jerome translated both testaments of Scripture into a new Latin version (AD 405) known as the *Vulgate*. It was the preferred Bible text throughout most of Europe for the next millennium. The Vulgate provides yet another test for the accuracy of the Old Testament.

## Dead Sea Scrolls

The discovery of the Dead Sea Scrolls starting in 1947 has proven to be the greatest manuscript discovery of modern times. A shepherd initially found clay jars in a cave a short distance from the Dead Sea. The jars contained leather scrolls with ancient Hebrew writing. Subsequently, manuscripts were found in eleven different caves. Cave four contained the majority of the manuscripts containing Scripture. Scholars were able to reconstruct more than five hundred books written in Hebrew, many of them containing large portions of the Old Testament. Only the book of Esther was missing from the scrolls. These ancient scrolls are from the first and second century BC, which is about a thousand years older than the earliest complete edition of the Masoretic text. They help confirm the overall accuracy of the Masoretic text. Most of the differences are insignificant.

## Ancient Copies of the New Testament

We have about five thousand ancient copies of portions of the New

Testament to examine and compare. Some of the earliest are third century AD translations of the New Testament into Old Latin, Syriac, and Egyptian. The Latin Vulgate and the Greek Codex Vaticanus, Codex Sinaiticus, and Codex Alexandrinus are all fourth and fifth century AD translations of the New Testament. We also have about seventy-five papyri fragments dating from 135 AD to the eighth century. Those fragments cover parts of all but two New Testament books. Overall, forty percent of the New Testament is covered by the early fragments.

4. How would you describe the amount of evidence we have to substantiate the New Testament text?

While it is true that no original New Testament manuscripts exist, the Bible scholars who work faithfully with the texts of those copies of manuscripts can compare the copies and determine what the words of the original manuscripts must have been. While not all scholars agree on how to prioritize the use of the manuscripts, the fact remains that about ninety percent of the New Testament is supported by all of the manuscripts. As with the Old Testament manuscripts, none of the major doctrines are affected where there are discrepancies in the New Testament texts. Critics simply cannot argue that our New Testament is invalid because we don't have enough evidence to establish an accurate text.

## Middle Ages

Literacy rates in Europe were around ten percent during the Middle Ages (AD 476 to fourteenth century). And the Bibles available at the time were mostly in Latin, a language only the church leadership understood. Stained glass and art in cathedrals were the closest the people came to understanding God's Word for themselves.

Near the end of the Middle Ages, an Oxford scholar and professor named John Wycliffe (1330–1384) became convinced that the contemporary Catholic church had drifted far from New Testament Christianity. He rightly believed the church was the people, and not the Catholic pope, priests, and sacramental system. If the people were going to understand the Bible and the distortions concerning the Catholic church, then they needed to at least have God's Word in their own language. Wycliffe earnestly desired that every common person *might learn the words of the Gospel according to his simplicity*. So he began to work on an English translation of the Latin Vulgate. He and his assistants completed a first edition before his death in 1384. Wycliffe's influence continued after his death prompting the Catholic church to condemn him as a heretic. His bones were dug up and crushed and his books were burned. The Wycliffe Bible was banned by church authorities and was frequently burned. In 1408 it became illegal to translate or read the Bible in vernacular English without permission from a bishop.

5. Why would the Catholic church be so interested in keeping the people from an English Bible? What were they afraid of losing?

As the Middle Ages were winding down and the Renaissance was beginning to spread across Europe, Johann Gutenberg greatly advanced Bible distribution with his development of the printing press in Germany (1453). The first book ever printed with the new invention was the Latin Vulgate version of the Bible. Later, German copies of the Scriptures were also printed on the new printing press.

## Reformation

The Catholic popes generally supported the return to the classic literature and art during the Renaissance, but they neither encouraged nor supported the growing availability of the Bible in the languages of the people. They wanted to maintain their authority over doctrine. In reality they frequently abused that right; they filled their coffers by selling God's forgiveness.

Martin Luther (1483–1546) nailed ninety-five theses to the Wittenberg church door in 1517 to communicate that the Bible, not the Catholic church, is the central religious authority and that salvation is by faith alone rather than by works. Because of Luther and others, Reformation teachings began to spread throughout Europe. Using the newly edited Greek text of Erasmus, Luther translated the New Testament into German in 1522 in an effort to allow the people to read the Bible for themselves. Twelve years later he finished his translation of the Old Testament.

## English Translations

In England, William Tyndale (c. 1494–1536), a chaplain and Oxford-trained scholar, had ambitions similar to those of the translators that came before him. After hearing an opponent say that it would be better to be without the Bible than it would to be without the pope's law, Tyndale retorted, *If God spare my life, ere many years I will cause a boy that driveth the plow to know more of the Scripture than thou dost.* Tyndale translated Erasmus's Greek New Testament into English by 1525, but he could not secure legal permission to print it in England. So he moved to the German provinces in order to print six thousand of them there (1526). English bishops bought up the Bibles and then burned them. But Tyndale simply used their money to fund a second edition (1534). He smuggled those Bibles into England in sacks of grain and flour. John Tewkesbury was arrested and burned at the stake for distributing Tyndale's New Testaments and for supporting Tyndale's belief in salvation by faith alone.

Tyndale finished translating fifteen Old Testament books before he was betrayed by a friend and arrested. His margin notes in his Old Testament translation were particularly condemning of the pope. In 1536 he was strangled and then burned. His greatest wishes while in prison were for warmer clothes and for the documents he needed in order to complete his translation of the Hebrew Old Testament into English. Apparently he received neither.

6. What is your reaction to Tewkesbury being burned at the stake and Tyndale being strangled and burned for making the Bible available to the common man?

7. How would you describe their actions that led to their deaths?

8. Read Philippians 1:21, 27–30. What similar approach to life do you see evident in the Apostle Paul's testimony?

Soon other English translations appeared including the Coverdale Bible, the first licensed Bible to be printed in English (1535). Miles Coverdale (c. 1488–1569) was exiled from England three times for his preaching against Catholic doctrine. The Matthew's Bible was produced in 1538. It was also a completed version of Tyndale's work. King Henry VIII eventually ordered a revision of the Matthew's Bible, called the Great Bible (1539), be placed in every church throughout England. The Great Bible was most notably missing the protestant notes found in the margins of the Matthew's Bible. The Great Bible also included an artistic cover page that put King Henry VIII as the center of attention. The picture was obviously meant to emphasize the importance of obeying the king. A picture of the prison was included on the page as a warning to those who didn't obey.

The Geneva Bible (1560) was the text carried to America by the Pilgrims in 1620. King James I of England did not like the Geneva Bible. He ordered another version of the Bible, the King James Version or Authorized Version. Forty-seven scholars worked on the translation over about three years. They consulted older translations, such as the Bishops' Bible and Tyndale's Bible, but they also labored over the original languages. The first copies of the new version came off the press in 1611. This original edition included variant readings and alternative translations in the margins.

Overall, the common English people were grateful to receive God's Word in their own language and enthusiastically purchased the new translations. Literacy rates began to climb during this same period. Many other English translations have been completed during the last century. These translations have a wide range of accuracy. The ones based on solid translation principles are most valuable.

## Principles for Translation Work

While a full explanation of principles for translation work would be rather detailed and lengthy, there are some general principles that we should be aware of.

Translators should have a high view of Scripture because the Bible is the inspired Word of God (2 Tim. 3:16). Inspiration, as we learned in an earlier chapter, includes the very words of the original autographs.

9. Read 2 Timothy 3:16. How will a translator who believes in the verbal inspiration of Scripture treat the words of Scripture he is translating into another language?

One well-established Bible translation ministry believes that translations should *express the very Word of God as literally as possible in the receptor languages without distorting, adding to, or obscuring the meaning of the original text*. What they describe is a *formal equivalence* method of translating the Bible. Others believe simply conveying the meaning, not the wording, of the text is all that is required of the translator. This method is called *dynamic equivalence*. Those who employ this method put an emphasis on *understanding* a passage rather than on conveying what the passage actually said. The problem with the dynamic equivalence method is that the translator actually plays the role of interpreter.

10. What are your thoughts on having the translator act as your interpreter of the Bible text?

Conservative scholars advocate that every word should be translated in a way that is literal and yet suitable in the new language. A suitable translation is structurally consistent with the receptor language and understandable to those who speak the language. An extremely wooden translation would not communicate the text very well in the receptor language. For example, a wooden translation of John 3:16 that would retain the same word order of the original Greek would awkwardly state: *Thus for He loved the God the world, that the Son the only-begotten He gave, in order that everyone the one believing into Him not may perish but may have life everlasting*. Obviously, Bible translators must arrange the translation in a manner that native speakers can comprehend.

Translators who espouse a more *dynamic equivalence* tend to be more idiomatic in an attempt to *smooth out* the translation. Consequently, some editions of the Bible are not really translations at all; they are paraphrases that provide a concept-by-concept gist of the original.

Bible translation is a difficult ministry. We should thank God that He not only gave us the original Scriptures, but that He also provided diligent servants to translate the Scriptures into the English language in a careful and accurate manner. Because of their work, we can be confident of the translation and understand what God is communicating through His Word.

## MAKING IT PERSONAL

Some believers don't talk about the Bible in public for fear someone might ridicule them. Such a *persecution* is a far cry from the price men like William Tyndale paid in order to share the Bible.

11. How openly do you share God's Word?

12. Describe how concerned you are that the lost have the opportunity to hear the gospel and read the Bible?

Take full advantage of the freedoms you enjoy to share God's Word openly. Pray you will have a burden to infuse God's Word into the lives of those who don't know God.

13. What might your church do to contribute to the distribution of God's Word around the globe?

# The Spirit's Illumination Ministry

## Scripture Focus

Gen. 3:8; John 20:30, 31; Rom. 1:18–32; 1 Cor. 2:9–16;
Eph. 4:18; 1 Tim. 2:3, 4; 2 Tim. 2:15; 1 John 5:13

## Theme

God gives believers the Holy Spirit to guide in understanding the Bible.

### Memory Verse

*"But the natural man receiveth not the things of the Spirit of God: for they are foolishness unto him: neither can he know them, because they are spiritually discerned"* (1 Corinthians 2:14).

## GETTING STARTED

Want to know when someone is perhaps not telling the truth? Watch their feet. When under stress, people will increasingly move their feet since they are not concentrating on their feet. Instead, they are concentrating on their facial expressions and arm movement to convince you they are telling the truth. So when you see someone's feet fidgeting, shuffling, winding around a chair, or even making quick moves as if they are ready to run, then you have good reason to question whether the person is being honest.

1. When have you suspected someone was not telling you the truth?

2. What tipped you off?

While feet might be indicators of a person's honesty, they are by no means a sure test of truthfulness. At best they would only raise questions. Some people approach the Word of God with the same level of uncertainty. They think that we can't be exactly sure what the Bible teaches. This lesson will address God's plan to communicate His truth to believers today.

## SEARCHING THE SCRIPTURES

### God Made People to Communicate

The Father, Son, and Holy Spirit have always communicated with One another because communication is an inseparable part of Their nature. And Their communication, in accordance with Their nature, is perfect; it is impossible for the members of the Godhead to miscommunicate.

3. Read Genesis 1:26. What did the persons of the Godhead talk about in this verse?

When Jesus came to earth, He continued to communicate with the Father. The Gospels give several examples of such communication.

4. Read Mark 1:35; Luke 6:12. How important was it for Jesus to communicate to the Father?

5. Read Matthew 26:36–44. What did Jesus communicate to the Father in the Garden of Gethsemane?

God desired to also interact with His creation, so He purposefully designed Adam in His image. Being in the image of God meant in part that Adam had the ability to communicate effectively, especially before the Fall. Adam could comprehend what God said to him and then respond in a way that God fully understood.

God created man to ultimately glorify Him (Eph. 1:3–14, *to praise of his glory*). That overarching goal necessitates that humanity have a means of understanding God objectively and then communicating to God based on that objective knowledge (1 Cor. 10:31). To know God objectively is to understand Him for Who He actually is. It is a knowledge free of bias and prejudice. Conversely, *subjective* knowledge is based on a biased, internal reality and doesn't necessarily represent truth. Some theologians question whether humans can actually have unbiased, objective knowledge of God based on His self-revelation in the Bible. But God would not be satisfied with a creation that related to Him only on a misguided subjective level. He had to provide a means for humanity to know the truth about Him so they could fulfill their ultimate purpose of actually glorifying Him.

## God Gave People His Word

Apparently God was in the habit of walking and talking with Adam and Eve in the Garden of Eden before Adam sinned. For after the Fall, Adam and Eve hid from God in an attempt to avoid what we could assume was one of God's regular appearances in Eden (Gen. 3:8). That God communicated with Adam and Eve before and after the Fall is clear from the creation account (1:28–30; 3:9–19). The Fall did dramatically affect Adam and Eve's relationship with God. They were no longer in fellowship with Him. They became sinners whose hearts and minds were darkened (1 Cor. 2:14). As a result, they had to leave the Garden of Eden, the place of their sweet communion with God (Gen. 3:24).

6. What topics do you suppose Adam asked God about before the Fall ruined his fellowship with God?

Adam and Eve needed God's direction for life even before the Fall (Gen. 1:28–30), so God revealed truth to Adam and Eve. And although it would be centuries before Scripture was formally recorded, God continued to reveal Himself and His truth to humanity after the Fall so that they might put their faith in Him and glorify Him (Heb. 1:1–3). Ultimately God used people to record His special revelation. As we studied in lesson 5, that special revelation has survived through the centuries so that our

Bibles today are rightfully called the Word of God. The testimony of the Bible is that God wants humanity to know Him and glorify Him (John 20:30, 31; 1 John 5:13). Those who refuse to put their faith in God and glorify Him are under His wrath. Paul wrote that those who observe God's creation are under condemnation for refusing to acknowledge God and glorify Him as creator (Rom. 1:18–32).

7. Read Romans 10:14–17. What is God's solution to unbelief?

God made His Word accessible. Those who hear or read the gospel message can understand its objective truth and respond to it by putting their faith in God (1 Tim. 2:3, 4). Once saved, the Word of God becomes a catalyst for the believer's spiritual growth (John 17:17; 1 Pet. 1:22—2:3).

But how can a believer ever really know that he is making proper sense of God's Word? How does he know when he has come to the right conclusions and has determined an accurate understanding for applying God's Word to his life?

God has designed a process to help us understand His Word. He has not left us on our own in hopes that we might somehow stumble onto a truth every once and a while. We can know the objective truth of God's Word. But knowing God's truth is not something that just happens to us. It takes action on our part.

## The Believer's Job

8. Read 2 Timothy 2:15. What does God expect the believer to do in order to properly understand God's Word?

Paul fully expected Timothy, a young preacher, to study the Word to the point of having his work acceptable to God. In fact, he phrased his expectation as a command: *Study to show thyself approved unto God*. Paul wouldn't command Timothy to do something that was impossible to do.

Timothy was to be a *workman* in the things of God, rightly dividing the Word of truth. *Rightly divide* means to *cut a straight line*. The word is used in a number of secular contexts: of making a road, of plowing a furrow, of constructing a stone wall or building. Perhaps the primary allusion in Paul's mind was the word's use in tent-making, for that was his occupation. Tents were made of animal hides and not of huge sheets of nylon, such as we have today. Several animal hides had to be cut straight so that one would butt up straight against the other and they could be stitched together to make the tent.

Likewise, the workman of God is to cut straight when handling the Word of God. That is, he is to interpret it correctly, understanding its various doctrines and seeing one Scripture in the light of other Scriptures so that all fits together into one harmonious whole. Many cults claim to base their teaching upon the Bible, but they isolate words or statements and give them a meaning which will not harmonize with the rest of the Bible. Then they produce a false teaching or cultic doctrine.

Today, the baseball is a perfect example of the importance of making sure two pieces of leather are lined up next to each other with no holes or overlaps. A pitcher must have a perfectly aligned baseball if his curve and slider are going to be effective. In the same way, a pastor needs to align the Scriptures as God intended if the Scriptures are going to be effective in his hands.

In order to rightly divide the Scriptures, Timothy needed to study. The word *study* means to *have diligence*, to *give haste*, or to *show eagerness*. It has been interpreted by the translators as *study* because the context is one of handling the Word. We ought to study it with diligence, not just when it happens to be convenient. We ought to study it with haste, not rushing through it but rushing to it. We ought to do it with eagerness and willingness. The results of such diligent study of the Word are correct understanding of its meaning and God's approval. God will examine the workman's work and declare it acceptable, or the workman will be put to shame.

The point we need to draw from Paul's instruction is that Timothy could actually teach and preach God's Word without being ashamed of having twisted and distorted its original meaning. He could preach and teach with confidence that he had interpreted and communicated God's Word as God intended. It is possible for us to do the same today. But diligent study of God's Word is needed.

So is accuracy in presenting God's Word based solely on the effort the teacher or preacher puts into the study? Is there another essential element in the process?

## The Spirit's Job

Diligent study of God's Word is only profitable because of the ministry of the Holy Spirit. The Spirit's job is to illuminate the Scriptures so the one diligently studying them can understand them properly. As mentioned above, the Fall left humanity with a mind darkened by sin (Eph. 4:18). The Bible calls the sinner the *natural* man (1 Cor. 2:14).

9. Read 1 Corinthians 2:14. What does the natural man, the unsaved person, conclude about the things of the Spirit of God?

The Bible essentially makes no sense to the unsaved person. The scientific method cannot uncover its truths. Higher education cannot fathom it. Nor can the human senses grasp it (1 Cor. 2:9). It is not that the natural man is stupid; he simply lacks the ministry of the Holy Spirit to enlighten his mind to understand the *things of the Spirit of God*. The *things* refer to what the Holy Spirit reveals to the believer about God through His Word.

10. How would you respond to a believer who says he doesn't read the Bible because he doesn't understand it?

All believers have the Spirit in them and therefore have the potential to study and understand God's Word. Bible study is for all believers because of the Spirit's presence with them. The Spirit enlightens their minds to grasp God's objective truth so they know for certain what the Bible says. Paul states in summary: *We have the mind of Christ* (1 Cor. 2:16). As we study God's Word, the Holy Spirit opens the eyes of our understanding. Our prayer should be: *Open thou mine eyes, that I may behold wondrous things out of thy law* (Ps. 119:18).

11. Share a time when you experienced your understanding of God's Word being opened for you. What was your reaction?

We should note that the person who studies God's Word will experience the Spirit's illumination so long as his heart is prepared properly. The believer who is living with known, unconfessed sin or who is simply going through the motions of Bible study out of a sense of duty will most likely will not gain from the Spirit's illuminating ministry. The Word of God is powerful enough, however, to convict both the sinning and the dutiful believer (Heb. 4:12).

Given the Spirit's illuminating ministry, why might anyone think that people cannot go to the Bible and be assured of objective truth? On what do they base their reasoning?

## Man's Problem with Communication

Skeptics question whether a person is even capable of reading the Bible and understanding it objectively. They wrongly focus on the limitations of humanity and overemphasize them to the point of doubting that objective truth from the Bible could ever be definitively known. In their estimation man is so influenced by his mind's flawed starting point that he could never understand the Bible. His subjective knowledge, what his mind thinks is reality, is an insurmountable barrier to understanding God's objective truth.

But those skeptics are frankly unbiblical in their thinking. What we just learned about the Spirit's illuminating ministry is the answer to man's inadequate, fallen, biased, prejudiced mind. The Spirit *is* the solution to the troubling consequences of the Fall. We can know God's objective truth because the Spirit is in us telling us what it is. We are not chained to our fallen, darkened minds because the chains are broken; we are new creations in Christ (2 Cor. 5:17). We can discern things that are spiritual and be absolutely certain of God's truth in His Word (1 Cor. 2:13, 14).

Other skeptics believe history proves that it is impossible for people to know God's objective truth from Scripture. They point to variations in interpretations between theologians as their evidence. When two theologians both claim their interpretation is right, the skeptics conclude that the interpretations are tainted by the theologians' limitations.

But an honest look at history reveals that those who adhere to the grammatical-historical principles for Bible interpretation almost always come to the same theological conclusions. The major doctrines in particular are well established historically. The historic establishment of doctrines is actually evidence that the Spirit's illuminating ministry overcomes the interpreter's human limitations.

We should never conclude that knowing God's Word is too hard or even impossible. God wants us to know Him through His Word so we might glorify His name. He gave us the Holy Spirit to make that possible. Let's let the Spirit work in us so we might know and live God's objective truth that we learn from God's Word.

## MAKING IT PERSONAL

12. Why might believers ignore the illuminating ministry of the Spirit?

13. Have you ever prayed that God would allow you to understand His Word? Explain.

14. How might such a practice change your reading and studying of the Bible?

15. How does the illuminating ministry of the Spirit fit with our fast-paced world?

16. How effective will the Spirit's illuminating ministry be if we treat the Bible like a book of soundbites?

There is no substitute for time in God's Word. There is no pill to take or magical shortcut. Even reading books by Christian authors is not a substitute for personal time in God's Word.

# Sola Scriptura

LESSON 7

## Scripture Focus

Deut. 4:2; Ps. 119:105; Prov. 30:5, 6; Matt. 4:1–11; 15:1–9; 2 Tim. 2:15; 3:16, 17; Rev. 22:18, 19

## Theme

God has no other authority for faith and practice besides the written Word of God.

### Memory Verses

*"But continue thou in the things which thou hast learned and hast been assured of, knowing of whom thou hast learned them; And that from a child thou hast known the holy scriptures, which are able to make thee wise unto salvation through faith which is in Christ Jesus."* (2 Timothy 3:14, 15).

## GETTING STARTED

A growing number of evangelicals are turning to Roman Catholic and Eastern Orthodox religions. They are intrigued by the liturgy, formality, and rituals. They feel the high church experience is more authentic and brings them closer to God. Furthermore, the high church doctrine appears more authoritative and true since both churches claim they are the successors to the apostolic church.

1. Does high church architecture and design appeal to you?

2. Why might someone think that such symbolism and design are signs of authenticity?

This study will help you see past the visual appeal of the high church architecture and design to consider why the Bible alone should be the basis of faith and practice.

## SEARCHING THE SCRIPTURES

### Views on the Authority of Scripture

The previous study examined the importance of the illuminating ministry of the Holy Spirit. This study will examine just what you should expect the Holy Spirit to illuminate. Some believe that the Bible is not our only source of authority and that the Spirit uses other sources to inform us on faith and practice.

The Latin phrase *sola scriptura* means *by Scripture alone*. The phrase is a way of stating that the Bible alone should determine our faith and practice. So those who hold to *sola scriptura* believe the Bible is the sole authority for what they believe and how they practice those beliefs. This study will give Biblical support for *sola scriptura*, a doctrine that has been under attack since the days of the apostles.

The Catholic Church and the Orthodox Church are the most prominent religions to add authoritative sources to the Bible. Both have a collection of writings from the church fathers, historical pronouncements, and official proclamations on doctrine. They call this collection their Tradition. They consider their Tradition as an authority equal to the Bible and consider it a means for interpreting the Bible. They believe their Tradition came from the oral teachings of Christ and the apostles and that God entrusted them with keeping that Tradition.

Furthermore, Catholics believe that God gave them *magisterium*, which they define as the divinely appointed authority to teach the truths of religion. Essentially the Catholic Church tells its followers what they are supposed to believe and do in order to be faithful to God. Exercising *magisterium* has resulted in many of the documents that make up Catholic Tradition. Both the Catholic and the Eastern Orthodox churches believe they have the supreme authority to interpret both the Bible and Tradition.

High church doctrine is not simply another viable option. It is actually deceptive and destructive. It is important for believers to understand the Biblical evidence for *sola scriptura*. Such an understanding helps us see that God provides all the truth we need in His written Word. The Bible is our sole authority for faith and practice. The high church experience is ultimately empty formalism that steers people away from God.

## Bible's Basis for Faith and Practice

The Bible's own testimony makes it clear that no other document or person is needed to establish God's truth for us. Second Timothy 3:16 is the central passage for establishing *sola scriptura*.

3. Read 2 Timothy 3:16, 17. What key words in these verses demonstrate that the Bible is sufficient for the believer?

God-breathed Scripture is sufficient for equipping the believer for every good work. And while *Scripture* in 2 Timothy 3:16 technically refers to the Old Testament, the New Testament is also called *Scripture* (2 Pet. 3:15, 16; 1 Tim. 5:18). Second Timothy 3:16 and 17 is essentially teaching that *all* of the Bible is inspired and sufficient. There is therefore no need for a second authority that has been passed down orally or otherwise.

## Jesus' Rebuke of Pharisaical Tradition

Furthermore, Jesus set Scripture above all other sources of authority, including the authority claimed by the Pharisees of His day (Matt. 15:1–9). The Pharisees believed they had received their tradition from Moses, supposedly making it as authoritative as the Scriptures Moses wrote. They complained that Jesus' disciples weren't following their traditions. In response, Jesus reproved the Pharisees, pointing out that they used their *tradition* to make the *commandment of God of none effect* (15:6). Instead of obeying Moses' written law and honoring their parents by caring for them (15:4; cf. Exod. 20:12; 21:17), they vowed to give all of their money as a gift to God (Matt. 15:5). In accordance with their traditions, they could not give their money to help their needy parents. In reality, the Pharisees were simply looking for a way to keep their money and use it as they wished so they wouldn't have to take care of their parents. They used their tradition to create a loophole around God's written Word.

The tradition the Pharisees appealed to is similar in nature to the tradition the Catholic and Orthodox churches appeal to today. All three are outside the Bible and all of them are or were used to reinterpret and even void the Bible. Jesus' rebuke of the religious leaders of His day could be appropriately applied to Catholic and Orthodox historical and present religious leaders.

In contrast to Jesus' rebuke of the Pharisaical tradition is His recognition of the Old Testament as the final and supreme authority. Jesus used the Old Testament when Satan tempted Him in the wilderness (Matt. 4:1–11). That Jesus quoted Scripture in one of His most intense experiences on earth is noteworthy.

4. Read Matt. 4:1–11. What was the result of Christ's use of Scripture to combat Satan's temptations?

In all, Jesus and the apostles quoted from or referred to the Old Testament nearly one hundred times. They repeatedly referred to that which was *written* (Mark 7:6, 7; 14:27; Rom. 3:4, 10). The *written* Word of God was authoritative for them. Eventually their use of the Old Testament also became part of God's Word when it was included in the inspired New Testament, leaving for us a testimony of the authority and sufficiency of the Bible.

## Bible's Warnings about Changing Scripture

Building off Jesus' rebuke of the Pharisees, the Bible directly addresses attempts to change the written Word of God. Catholic and Orthodox traditions are essentially additions to the Word of God.

5. Read Deuteronomy 4:2. What did Moses warn concerning the commands God gave through him?

Agur wrote that the Word of God's pureness is like that of a perfectly refined metal (Prov. 30:5).

6. Read Proverbs 30:5, 6. What would be true of the person who tried to add to God's Word?

The apostle Paul wrote to Corinth to tell them that they needed to stick with what the Scriptures say and not to develop their own standards by which to judge men (1 Cor. 4:6). John was even more emphatic in his warning that closed out the book of Revelation (Rev. 22:18, 19).

7. Read Revelation 22:18, 19. How serious was John's warning?

John's warning essentially says that changing God's Word is evidence that a person has rejected God. No one who rejects God will experience the joys of Heaven.

Many Catholics and Orthodox Christians are trusting in their works to earn grace for salvation. They are basing that trust on doctrines that are in turn based on traditions outside of God's Word. Catholics and Orthodox Christians have rejected God's Word and His way of salvation. They are still lost in their sins.

## Inclusion of Apostolic Writings in the Canon

The clear warnings about adding to or subtracting from Scripture applied to the apostles too. Just because God communicated the New Testament through them didn't give them the authority to write something on their own and claim it as Scripture. In fact, none of them did that. Their inspired writings were recorded as Scripture and eventually recognized as part the New Testament Canon. But there were no further writings or oral traditions that emerged from the first century apostles that were later recognized as authoritative additions to the completed New Testament. Every apostle obeyed God's instructions about not adding to the Word of God.

The New Testament does talk about *traditions* from the apostles. Their teachings and writings made up their traditions, but not everything they said or wrote was considered God's inspired Word. They spoke authoritatively because they had been ordained by God as leaders in the establishment of Christ's church (Acts 2:42; Eph. 2:20). The apostle Paul even told believers to *keep* the traditions (1 Cor. 11:2) and *hold* them (2 Thess. 2:15). As mentioned, what is the inspired Word of God was recorded and eventually recognized as such. *Tradition* was a general term for describing what the apostles taught and passed down. When they died, their authority lived on in the inspired books they wrote. Nothing else they said or wrote was perpetuated as inspired. There is nothing missing from our New Testament. It is complete and sufficient for us.

8. Read John 20:30; 21:25. What was John's testimony concerning the record of all that Christ said and did?

Certainly everything Jesus taught was perfectly true and worth knowing. But most of it was not recorded in the Bible. Yet we aren't lacking anything God wanted us to know about Christ actions and teachings. The same is true of the apostles.

## God's Commands concerning Revelation

A *written* Word was God's plan all along. We find many times throughout the Bible that He commanded His Word to be written down. Conversely, we don't find similar commands for God's Word to be kept as an oral tradition and left unwritten. It simply doesn't make any sense for God to leave part of His authoritative Scripture in an unwritten form.

9. Read Deuteronomy 31:26. What was done with Moses' Book of the Law before he died?

10. Read Joshua 24:25, 26. Why was it important for Joshua to record the people's covenant?

Samuel wrote the instructions for the king of Israel (1 Sam. 10:25). It most likely included the Mosaic Law's instructions for royalty as recorded in Deuteronomy 17:14–20.

11. Read Isaiah 30:8, 9. Why did God want Isaiah to record His message?

As mentioned earlier, Jesus and the New Testament writers often quoted from the Old Testament writings. Obviously the written Word of God was authoritative for them.

12. Read Matt. 22:29. Why did Jesus condemn the Jewish religious leaders?

The testimony of Scripture is clear. God wanted His revelation written down and then expected the writings to be respected and treated as His Word. The question is whether the written Word of God is understandable. Do we need additional revelation to even know what the Bible says?

## Bible's Perspicuity

*Perspicuous* is the word we use to communicate that the Bible is understandable. It means *clear* and *comprehensible*. The Bible has perspicuity in that its message is abundantly clear. It does not need additional documents, pronouncements, or traditions to communicate its obvious message. When a person reads it, there are transformative results. It is accessible and intelligible. Its teaching is direct and complete. Scripture is clear in what it addresses, though that does not mean every passage is easy to understand (2 Pet. 3:16). Understanding certain passages demands careful study. But the fact that there are challenging passages does not mean the Bible is not perspicuous. The failure is not in the clarity of the Bible but in the ability or fault of the person reading it.

Catholics don't believe the Bible has perspicuity. They add their oral tradition to the Bible's teaching and employ their *magisterium* to interpret it authoritatively, claiming no one could fully understand the Bible without their God-ordained help. They essentially point to documents outside the Bible as evidence that the Bible is not perspicuous. But proving the Bible's perspicuity should begin by looking inside the Bible rather than outside the Bible. If the Bible is perspicuous, then there is no need to look for another source of authoritative revelation. The Bible's perspicuity would effectively eliminate the need for both an oral tradition and a God-ordained *magisterium*.

13. If the Bible were not perspicuous, then what would stop anyone from claiming he is the one who has the additional revelation from God to help in interpreting the Bible?

Lesson two presented the case for the inspiration of Scripture, demonstrating that all of Scripture as recorded by the original authors is inspired and profitable for spiritual growth (2 Tim. 3:16, 17). The fact that the Bible is inspired by the Holy Spirit means it is ludicrous to think that it is somehow deficient. Why would God give only part of the His body of truth in written form, relegating other parts to oral traditions? Such a plan would make no sense practically and would open up the body of God's revelation to serious error. In fact, that is what has happened. The Catholic Church has used their self-proclaimed authority over the Bible as a means of perverting what are otherwise clear doctrines in the Bible. And the history of the Catholic Church is replete with convenient doctrinal changes that at times helped them fill their coffers and grab political power.

This study has also already addressed the illuminating ministry of the Holy Spirit (lesson 6). In part, it is the Spirit's ministry on behalf of believers that makes the Bible perspicuous. As a believer is diligent to study God's Word, the Holy Spirit will provide understanding so that the individual believer rightly interprets and applies the Word (2 Tim. 2:15).

Furthermore, the Bible calls itself a *light*. Such figurative language supports the Bible's perspicuity.

14. Read Psalm 119:105. What does this verse reveal about the purpose of God's Word?

God's intention was to clearly communicate His truth in His Word so that it would be our guide for life. It would make no sense for God to give us a *light* that was not sufficient for illuminating all we need to know about living for God.

## MAKING IT PERSONAL

15. How confident are you that the Scriptures are the sole authority for faith and practice?

16. Do you ever wish you could get a set of cliff notes on the Bible that would be an official commentary to help you understand it all? Explain.

Remember the previous study about the illumination ministry of the Holy Spirit and be patient as you study God's Word and learn its truth. It is truly an astounding Book. The more you get to know it, the more you will appreciate just how expertly and coherently it is written and just how powerfully it can affect your life.

17. How intriguing is the high church atmosphere to you in light of the evidence for sola scriptura?

18. What evidence for the Bible's authority helps you see the folly of high church doctrine?

19. What might you do to prepare yourself to help friends and family members who are intrigued with or involved in Catholicism or Eastern Orthodoxy?

# Required Principles of Interpretation

LESSON 8

## Scripture Focus

2 Kings 22:8–20; Ps. 19:7–11; John 17:17; 2 Tim. 3:16, 17; 1 Pet. 5:6

## Theme

God expects believers to interpret the Bible carefully so that they might learn His truth in His Word.

**Memory Verse**

*"For Ezra had prepared his heart to seek the law of the LORD, and to do it, and to teach in Israel statutes and judgments"*

*(Ezra 7:10).*

## GETTING STARTED

Some people like to read the end of a book before reading the rest of the story. Doing so opens the door for grave misunderstanding. For the reader will draw conclusions about the story and characters based on a passage out of the context of the rest of the book.

1. Have you ever read the end of a book before reading the rest of it?

2. If so, how did your perception about the ending change once you read the rest of the book?

You learned in lesson six that the Holy Spirit helps you understand the Bible as you are diligent to study it. Lesson seven presented the case for *sola scriptura*. This study will help you understand principles for interpreting Scripture. One of those principles is to study a passage in its context, a rule that keeps you from misunderstanding and misapplying a passage.

## SEARCHING THE SCRIPTURES

### Presuppositions to Bible Interpretation

*Presuppositions* are the implicit assumptions we make before embarking on a study, investigation, or dialogue. Our presuppositions guide our worldviews and give us a framework for understanding what we observe. Before we embark on Bible interpretation, it is good to understand the presuppositions that should guide our process.

First, we need to recognize that God has provided objective truth for us in His Word (Ps. 19:7–11). That means we should expect to find *the* truth (John 17:17) in the Bible rather than *our* truth. God's Word does not exist for us to twist and bend in order to create our own truth.

Second, we need to understand that God's truth neither changes nor contradicts itself. It is not subject to our opinions and feelings. Instead, God's Word is authoritative. It is the *final* word and the only word that really matters. That means we ought to approach God's Word with humility, submitting ourselves to its supreme authority and sanctifying effects (2 Tim. 3:16, 17; 1 Pet. 5:6).

3. Given these presuppositions, what should our goal be as we seek to interpret the Bible?

King Josiah provides an excellent example of having correct presuppositions about God's Word and then responding to God's Word accordingly.

4. Read 2 Kings 22:8–13. Based on Josiah's actions, what would you say were his presuppositions concerning the Book of the Law (the Pentateuch)?

5. Read 2 Kings 22:14–17. Why might Josiah have ignored or discredited God's Word? Consider Judah's situation at that time.

6. Read 2 Kings 22:18–20. How did Josiah personally respond to the Book of the Law?

The presuppositions that God's Word is true, accessible, and unchangeable are foundational. They set up the Word as our authority on all that the Bible reveals. So with these foundational presuppositions in mind, we need to be aware of the principles for studying and understanding God's Word.

There are certain principles that should guide our Bible interpretation. We must observe them without wavering if we are to arrive at a correct understanding of the Scriptures.

## Interpret Literally

The first principle of sound Bible interpretation is to interpret Scripture literally. *Literal* interpretation means a straightforward, normal reading of the text. It includes the realization that normal language employs the use of figures of speech. So literal interpretation recognizes the need to interpret the figurative language in a figurative sense.

7. Read Psalm 23. What are some of the truths David communicated by his figurative speech in this psalm?

8. Read John 6:35. What did Jesus mean when He called Himself the bread of life?

*Literal* interpretation is the term used in opposition to *spiritual* or *allegorical* interpretation. It is important to understand the difference, starting with the origin of the two methods of interpretation.

Literal interpretation was practiced by Jesus and the New Testament writers, who interpreted the Old Testament in a literal sense (Matt. 4:4, 7, 10; Luke 4:16–21; Rom. 3:10–18). The early church continued to use literal interpretation until around AD 135 when Jewish pastors were replaced by Greek pastors in Jerusalem. Eventually the Greek pastors were influenced by Greek thought, particularly when Augustine began promoting spiritual interpretation in the fourth century AD.

*Spiritual* interpretation has its origins several hundred years before Augustine. Plato, a Greek philosopher from the fifth and fourth centuries BC, developed a non-literal method of interpreting Greek religious writings in order to avoid the embarrassment of the Greek gods' immoral behavior recorded in those writings. Plato believed the religious documents were actually meant to point the reader to a deeper *spiritual* meaning. So the non-literal, allegorical interpretation was called the *spiritual* interpretation. Today, *spiritual* interpretation means taking the words of a Bible text and treating them as if they were merely a metaphor or allegory for some meaning obscured or hidden behind the literal text.

Some Bible passages seem to be figurative when they are not. So the interpreter needs to be careful. For instance, God's promises about the future city of Jerusalem appear to be figurative (Isa. 60:10–21). Yet there is no reason to consider them anything less than literal.

9. Read Isaiah 60:10–21. What are some of the prophecies about a future, glorious day for the city of Jerusalem?

When Isaiah 60:10–21 is interpreted literally, it helps to solidify the testimony of God's faithfulness to Israel, which in turn builds the reader's confidence in God's faithfulness to him. A literal interpretation also provides an accurate understanding about Israel's future.

## Discover the Authorial Intent

In a world that is increasingly driven by political correctness, people are hesitant to tell others when their opinion is wrong. But when it comes to interpreting Scripture, everyone is *not* entitled to his own opinion. So beginning a group Bible study by asking everyone to share what a passage means to them is potentially disastrous. Most likely people in the Bible study group will share errant interpretations. Some will frankly say what they *want* the passage to mean because the meaning is convenient for them and fits their needs at that point in their life. But Bible study is not about projecting one's personal interpretation onto a text.

Bible study is about discovering the *author's* intent. A passage can have more than one appropriate application, but it can have only *one* meaning. The single meaning of a text must be determined on the basis of what the original author intended it to mean. Determining author intent is of high importance for accurate interpretation.

We practice the rule of determining author intent every time we read a new article. For example, if a news reporter wrote *three people died in a plane crash*, we would not understand it to mean that the author was using a plane crash to tell us that *three people had their dreams come crashing to earth*. Text has meaning, and the meaning is to be determined by what the original author intended. Based on that single meaning, we may be able to determine multiple applications to our lives. Too often, in our haste to make the Bible relevant to our lives, we skip the work of determining the meaning of the text, and go right to trying to determine the application.

10. What is so tempting about applying a passage before a person knows the author's intent for the passage?

There are actually some academics who argue for the legitimacy of multiple meanings for written texts. This theory of linguistics is known as the *Reader Response Theory*. One area where we see this played out in America is in how some legal experts interpret the US Constitution. They view it as a fluid or living document. They believe the meaning of the Constitution can change from what its authors originally intended. This kind of legal reasoning is used to justify certain interpretations of the Constitution that run contrary to a strict constitutionalist approach.

Of course with this approach, one could get the Constitution to mean just about anything, effectively rendering the Constitution worthless. Much the same thing happens when it comes to the Bible. There are strict literalists who hold to a single meaning of the Bible, and there are those who believe that the Bible is a living document whose meaning can change in different times and cultures.

11. How would your view of the Bible change if it was a fluid document with changing meanings?

Some theologians are also guilty of violating the principle of single meaning. They do so to advance their theological understanding of the Bible. Covenant theologians, for example, find second meanings for passages on Israel and the future kingdom because an earthly, millennial Kingdom of Christ is not part of their theological understanding. In Luke 1:32 and 33 the angel Gabriel told Mary that Jesus *shall be great, and shall be called the Son of the Highest: and the Lord God shall give unto him the throne of his father David: And he shall reign over the house of Jacob for ever; and of his kingdom there shall be no end.* Luke obviously meant that Jesus will sit on a literal throne in Jerusalem ruling over the nation of Israel (the house of Jacob). Covenant theologians believe the passage can mean that Jesus will sit on a heavenly throne ruling in the hearts of Christians who have trusted Him as Savior. In this case, Luke's intent could not have been to communicate both meanings because both can't be right. Luke's message means only what the angel intended for Mary to understand by these words. Mary's understanding was undoubtedly based on what Mary knew from the Old Testament Scriptures and specifically the Davidic Covenant recorded in 2 Samuel 7 and Psalm 89. The Davidic Covenant promised that Israel's Messiah would come from the descendants of David and that he would rule over the nation of Israel.

Finding a meaning to fit one's theological understanding is not appropriate Bible interpretation. Sound interpreters will let the clear authorial intent dictate the meaning of the text.

## Consider Context

There is no greater principle of interpretation than this: Any text of Scripture must be understood based on how it is used in its context. Context includes the immediate verses, the chapter, the book, and even the entire Bible. That is why the more familiar we become with the whole Bible, the more equipped we will be to understand the books, chapters, and verses of the Bible.

Context is often a crucial determiner of the correct meaning of a text. One can appear to prove most anything from the Bible by yanking verses out of context. Philippians 4:13 provides an example of the need to consider context before drawing conclusions about a text.

12. Read Philippians 4:13. What does this verse appear to mean?

Some people have used Philippians 4:13 to justify some fantastic claims. What did Paul mean by *all things*? Did he mean that he could swim across the Mediterranean Sea without drowning? Most likely you wouldn't agree to such an application, but how would you know? Context tells us.

13. Read Philippians 4:10–19. What do you notice about the context around verse 13?

There is a paragraph that begins in verse 10 and ends with verse 13. The paragraph divisions in the Bible are the result of the translators' judgment; they are not inspired. However, they are worth heeding in the initial phases of the study. In the context of the paragraph, we observe that the Philippians had shown concern for Paul's circumstances. According to verse 12, his circumstances included both poverty and plenty. In reading verses 14 through 19, the paragraph that follows verse 13, it becomes clear that the Philippians had shown their concern by sending a financial gift to support Paul's ministry. That relieved a difficult situation and allowed Paul to be fully supplied (4:18). And though Paul had been in need before their gift arrived (4:11, 12), he had still served Christ. After his need was met plentifully, he planned to continue to serve Christ. His contentment was not based on his circumstances. Christ was his strength, whether he had much or whether he had little. The apostle Paul could do everything necessary to serve Christ because Christ would strengthen him to keep on in poverty or in plenty. So *I can do all things* is defined by its context to include all things that involve service for Christ no matter what the circumstances. Observing the context leads us to understand the true meaning of the passage.

Part of considering context is to let Scripture interpret Scripture. This rule might seem unnecessary, if we assume that all Scripture is plain and easy to understand. But there are plenty of Bible passages that are difficult to interpret. Turning to other Scriptures for information on how to interpret a difficult passage is essentially considering the passage's greater context. And since the Bible does not contradict itself, consulting the rest of the Bible in order to shed light on a difficult passage is the most accurate way to interpret the passage.

Unfortunately, many false doctrines have been birthed from misinterpretations of difficult passages or passages that are not immediately clear. For example, the Mormons use Ezekiel 37:15–17 to teach that God planned for the Book of Mormon and that He recognizes it as equal to the Bible.

14. Read Ezekiel 37:15–17. What would you think this passage is about without reading its context?

The Mormons believe that the two sticks are two scrolls which were rolled up on sticks and then joined. They say the first scroll represents the Bible and the second scroll represents the Book of Mormon. Obviously this passage is crucial to their belief that the Book of Mormon was ordained by God.

15. Read Ezekiel 37:18–22. What explanation does the context provide for this obscure passage?

God wanted Ezekiel to use the two sticks as visual aids in talking about the future for the divided kingdoms of Judah and Israel (Ephraim). Eventually God was going to join the two kingdoms together again. The passage, when considered in its context, has nothing at all to do with scrolls or books. The Mormons have committed an egregious violation of the rules of interpretation and have led millions of people astray because of it.

Any interpretation of a difficult passage must align with what we know to be true in the passage's immediate context and the rest of the Bible. Using an obscure passage out of context in order to create a new doctrine is wrong. God is not pleased when people get creative with His Word and use it to back their own teachings.

## MAKING IT PERSONAL

16. Do your Bible study habits make you prone to misinterpreting Scripture? Explain.

17. What might you do to make your study more careful?

18. What might your church do to foster careful study of God's Word?

19. How might you express your gratitude to your pastor for being a careful interpreter of God's Word?

# The Powerful Sword



## Scripture Focus

Matt. 4:1–11; Rom. 1:16–31; 12:1, 2; Eph. 4:21; 6:10–17

## Theme

God's Word is a powerful discerner and defender.

### Memory Verses

*"With my whole heart have I sought thee:*
*O let me not wander from thy commandments.*
*Thy word have I hid in mine heart, that I might not sin against thee"*
*(Psalm 119:10, 11).*

## GETTING STARTED

Every moment of everyday there are military personal at the ready to launch missiles against any nation that is attacking the United States or its allies. The power at the fingertips of those military personnel is staggering to think about.

1. What is the most power you have ever had at your fingertips?

2. Describe your respect for the power you wielded?

This study takes a step back from the more academic study of the Bible to consider its power in our lives. In reality, we could all say that the Bible is the most powerful thing we have had at our fingertips.

## SEARCHING THE SCRIPTURES

The Bible addresses humanity's basic need for salvation. Romans 1, Paul's letter on salvation, begins with the Word's power to meet that need.

### The Power of God for Salvation

Romans 1 demonstrates that every person is a sinner in need of God's grace and that everyone who rejects God's grace is condemned by God and subject to His wrath. In Romans 1:18, the word *suppress* better expresses the meaning of the word translated *hold*. The verse refers to people who have the truth about God but refuse to acknowledge it. Thus, God's wrath falls on them.

3. Read Romans 1:18–20. Why does no one have an excuse for not knowing God?

To create anything as large as the earth—and beyond that the heavens—requires unfathomable power. Everyone should readily recognize that there must be a creator who is infinitely powerful and wise and far above humanity (Ps. 19:1–4).

Knowing about God does not, by itself, save anyone. The Bible teaches that there is no *other name under heaven given among men, whereby we must be saved* (Acts 4:12). Those who do not believe in Christ are condemned because they have not believed in the name of the only begotten Son of God (John 3:18). Salvation depends upon knowing and trusting in Jesus Christ. Special revelation (the Word of God and its teaching on the Savior) is necessary for the lost to know and trust Christ. And the special revelation in God's Word is sufficient.

Another reason for God's wrath is that people have a knowledge of God but do not respond properly to it (Rom. 1:21–25). When people reject the light of natural revelation of God, they in effect say that the revelation is false. They then become *vain in their imaginations* (1:21), meaning their reasoning becomes futile. Their hearts become darkened so that they reject God (Eph. 4:18). They become fools (Rom. 1:22), thinking their understanding of life is right. As fools they descend into idolatry, worshiping what God created instead of God (1:23, 25).

The key words in verse 24 are *God also gave them up*. If people set themselves on a certain course and will not turn from it, God allows them to go that way and suffer the consequences. If people abandon God, they abandon their only hope.

Romans 1:26–32 describes the downward spiral of those who reject God. They end up as one with a *reprobate mind* (1:28) who is unable to discern the difference between right and wrong. After the mind has been distorted, the body becomes debased too (1:29–31).

4. Read Romans 1:29–31. What is your impression when you read this list? Are you surprised by some of the sins listed as being part of humanity's abandonment of God? Explain.

Paul's description of humanity is rather grim. Humanity is lost and without any desire or power to come to God for salvation. But God's Word brings the power to change their hearts and minds so they might see their need for a Savior and respond.

5. Have you ever thought that someone was so lost in his sins that there was no way he would ever respond to the gospel? Explain.

## The Word's Powerfulness

We need to back up in Romans 1 to catch Paul's introduction to his extended statement on humanity's lostness. He began his statement with a simple declaration of the gospel's power. Paul wrote that the gospel is *the power of God unto salvation* (1:16).

The Bible is our only source for the story of the unfolding of the gospel. To consider the power of the gospel, then, is to consider the power of the Word of God. As the gospel is shared from God's Word, God exercises its power to save those who are powerless to save themselves. God's power is effective for everyone who believes in His Son for salvation (1:16).

Paul was not ashamed of the gospel because it works! The gospel is the power of God unto salvation. Paul himself was *Exhibit A*. Even the Christians found it hard to believe that Saul of Tarsus, the persecutor and ruthless killer, was converted (Acts 9:26). But the mighty gospel of God had transformed his life, and he knew it would do the same for others.

In this powerful gospel, *the righteousness of God* is revealed (1:17). Righteousness is being right and doing right by God's standards. To be righteous is to be upright, just. The condition for receiving this righteousness is *faith* in Christ. The believer then exercises his faith to grow in Christ.

## The Power of God for Sanctification

God's Word is essential for believers who want to grow in Christ. Spiritual growth cannot happen apart from God's Word.

In the Old Testament, the people of Israel fell into unfaithfulness because they acted on the basis of their feelings rather than by faith. God had given them His clear word that they were to enter Canaan. He asked them to trust Him, obey His instructions, and enter His promised rest. But rather than grasping the challenge in the light of God's promises, they avoided the challenge because it seemed too great for them (Num. 14:1–4). Israel's mistake came in replacing God's fixed standard of His word with the flawed standard of their perspectives and feelings. Only God's truthful Word can give His people a reliable guide for life.

In Hebrews 4:12 the writer described the Word of God. It is quick, or alive. It is powerful, unlike the timid fear of people. It is more incisive than any sword designed by men, because it can penetrate into even the deepest parts of a person's immaterial life. God's Word critiques even the most hidden thoughts and intentions that people have. It can expose all pretenses, excuses, and inconsistencies.

6. Read Hebrews 4:12, 13. How do these two verses demonstrate the unity between the Word of God and the person of God?

Even Christians can deceive themselves into disobeying God's Word. They may rationalize their sinful choices, but they cannot fool God. No one can avoid His searching gaze (4:13). God is a light that illumines every action, desire, and motive. When excuses for disobedience are examined in the light of God and His Word, they always prove to be foolish.

7. What rationalizations might some people give for their sins?

No circumstances can justify disobedience. No fear will make sin acceptable to God. He has spoken in His Word, and He demands that people live by it if they are to enjoy His blessing.

Some people are ignorant of what God has said. Others, such as most of the Israelites and some who profess to be Christians, have learned God's Word, but they do not respond to it with faith. In both cases, God's Word is the standard for human behavior. Only those people who learn what God has said and do what He desires can enjoy the blessing of fellowship with Him. God's Word is His essential instruction for human beings. It shows us both where we are wrong and what is right (cf. 2 Tim. 3:16, 17).

While the Bible exposes our sins and shines the light on God's standard of holiness, it also provides us with victory over temptations to violate that standard. The Word is vital for victorious Christian living.

## Jesus' Pattern

Jesus provides us with an example of the connection between God's Word and victory over temptation.

Near the start of His earthly ministry, Jesus went into the wilderness to fast and pray. His meat was the will of God (John 4:34), and the living water of the Holy Spirit's presence in His prayer life sustained Him and prepared Him for the contest with Satan. After forty days, Satan showed up to tempt Him. Jesus faced the temptations, using God's Word as His tool.

Going without food for forty days takes an incredible amount of strength and fortitude. The normal human response to such prolonged food depravation is severe weight loss, pain, extreme listlessness, and confusion. So Satan started with offering Jesus food. In response Jesus directly addressed the real issue: *It is written, Man shall not live by bread alone, but by every word that proceedeth out of the mouth of God* (Matt. 4:4; cf. Deut. 8:3). What God says is more important than what Satan says and more important than what our own needs and desires tell us. God's will should always determine the choices we make.

Jesus Christ refused to satisfy His physical need for food outside the will of God. Had He yielded to that temptation, He would have disqualified Himself from being the Savior of the world. Of course that was never a possibility. Jesus couldn't sin because He is the perfect Son of God.

8. Satan attacks humanity using the lust of the flesh. What is the universal record for all humanity in facing temptations that appeal to the lust of the flesh?

Having failed in his first attempt to entice Jesus away from His program of ministry, Satan shifted his attack to something more precious to Jesus than the satisfaction of physical needs. Satan took Him to the temple in Jerusalem, the heart of worship and service to God and the highest point in the city. Acknowledging that Jesus is the Son of God and therefore in a special relationship to God, Satan urged Him to throw Himself down from the temple in a demonstration of His trust in God (Matt. 4:5, 6). It was a subtle, clever suggestion, underlined with a passage of Scripture. Jesus had used the Old Testament, and Satan began to argue from the same basis.

Satan's second test of Christ probed His confidence in God: *Cast Yourself down; You're the Son of God. It will be a miraculous display of Your relationship to the Father as we see God take care of You.* The Jews expected the Messiah to come in a spectacular way: *The Lord, whom ye seek, shall suddenly come to his temple* (Mal. 3:1). Here was an opportunity for Jesus to announce the beginning of His ministry in a dramatic way and thereby gain the attention and support of the leaders of the temple and the city. But daring God by putting oneself deliberately in danger is not trusting God. We do not invite trouble just to claim God's protection.

Jesus quoted Deuteronomy 6:16, saying, *It is written again, Thou shalt not tempt [test] the Lord thy God* (Matt. 4:7). He emphasized that Scripture is more than occasional texts. God's words are not to be used out of context to support someone's desires. Jesus did not need a miracle to prove that He had confidence in God.

9. Satan seemed to be looking out for Jesus by giving Him an opportunity to get ahead. Satan does the same to us. Why is that wily tactic so effective?

The vision of a worldwide network of lands and people in a unified government has been the goal of a number of ambitious leaders. Jesus of Nazareth, descendant of King David, would be eligible to assume the throne of a united Israel and restore the nation's ancient glory. Satan supposed that having that position, plus making Israel the head of all the nations and ruling them, would appeal to Jesus. Showing Christ all these kingdoms, he made to Jesus the grandiose offer of all the kingdoms of the world if He would just acknowledge Satan as an object of worship (4:8, 9). Satan was offering a compromise; the kingdoms came with a price tag: Satan would retain his position, and Jesus would worship him. He could have the kingdoms without the cross. But no one can serve two masters (6:24), and we must worship the one we serve.

Satan's offer provided immediate authority over kingdoms, but Psalm 2 draws a more accurate picture of the prospect for world leadership. God has promised the uttermost parts of the earth for the Son's possession. The psalm advises the kings and judges to serve the Lord with fear: *Kiss the Son, lest he be angry, and ye perish from the way* (Ps. 2:12). Jesus answered, *It is written* and then ordered Satan to leave. The Devil left for a season, defeated but not destroyed.

Jesus' victory over temptation was dependent on the Word of God. He quoted Scripture because it has power. In a real sense, God's Word was a sword in the Son of God's hand. The apostle Paul actually calls the Word of God a *sword*, and adds that the Holy Spirit is the One Who wields it with precision and power.

## The Spirit's Precision

In His letter to the church at Ephesus, the apostle Paul used armor as a metaphor for the believer's defense against Satan's wily ways (Eph. 6:10–17). The *helmet of salvation* is the last defensive piece of armor Paul mentioned (6:17). Since he was addressing Christians, he did not use the word *salvation* in the sense of the saving of one's soul. By *salvation* he meant present deliverance from the power of Satan and sin. Just as a helmet protects a soldier's head, so the helmet of salvation protects the mind from the destructive philosophies and attitudes that Satan launches at us.

10. Read Romans 12:1, 2. What is the connection between right thinking and right living?

11. Read Ephesians 4:21. Paul took time to teach the Ephesians. How did Paul summarize what he taught them?

Our fight against Satan and the hosts of evil includes offensive strategy as well as defensive strategy. We must invade his territory. Paul described our offensive weapon as *the sword of the Spirit, which is the word of God* (Eph. 6:17). The Christian's sword is the Bible. We must become so well acquainted with Scripture that we can draw upon just the right verse at the right time to ward off an attack by the Devil.

A Roman soldier used his sword to parry a blow from an opponent's sword and to strike a blow at the enemy. The Christian's sword is the *sword of the Spirit* because it is the Holy Spirit Who inspired the Bible and uses God's Word to accomplish God's purposes in our lives. When we attempt to invade Satan's territory, we must be well armed with Scripture. It is God's help to us in living victorious over temptation for the glory of God.

## MAKING IT PERSONAL

12. What will characterize a person's use of God's Word once he recognizes its power to discern and defend?

13. How have you treated God's Word: as a regular book or as a powerful weapon?

14. What will you do to unleash the power of the Bible in your life?

15. How might your church unleash the power of the Bible in its ministries?

# Old Testament Books

LESSON 10

## Scripture Focus

Various Bible passage

## Theme

God inspired each book of the Old Testament with purpose and for our benefit.

**Memory Verse**

*"Now all these things happened unto them for examples: and they are written for our admonition, upon whom the ends of the world are come" (1 Corinthians 10:11).*

## GETTING STARTED

Perhaps nothing motivates a person more to actually read a book than being in a book club. It is impossible to contribute to an analysis of a book you've never read.

1. Have you ever tried to fake your way through a book club meeting?

2. How do you think you would fare if you were to attend a book club about the Minor Prophets?

This study will give an overview of each of the Old Testament books and will encourage you to be familiar with the whole Bible, even the Minor Prophets.

## SEARCHING THE SCRIPTURES

### The Books of the Law

The books of the law contain the Law of Moses, but they also include a lot of narrative. Narratives are primarily accounts of how God dealt with humanity. We need to look for God in every account we study. His dealings with humanity will almost always translate to some degree into our lives today.

**Genesis.** Genesis takes us back to the beginning of time when God created the heavens and the earth in a six-day period. Genesis also relates how mankind fell into sin and was driven out of the Garden of Eden by God. In addition, Genesis describes the Flood and the family and call of Abraham. Genesis spans a longer period of time than all the rest of the Bible put together. It begins at Creation and ends with the family of Jacob living in Egypt, approximately 1800 BC.

**Exodus.** *Exodus* means *a way out*. This book tells how God used Moses to lead the Israelites out of Egyptian bondage, and how He gave Moses the Ten Commandments at Mount Sinai (20). Exodus also mentions God's detailed instructions about the tabernacle and directions concerning the priesthood.

**Leviticus.** The book of Leviticus deals primarily with Aaron and his sons. It includes material on priestly consecration and an example of judgment on those who take God lightly. Nadab and Abihu (two of Aaron's sons) were struck dead for not following God's instructions concerning the fire on the altar. Leviticus closes with regulations concerning property dedicated to God.

**Numbers.** The book of Numbers receives its name from a census taken of Israel (3:15). Though Numbers is one of the five books of the Law, it is more history than legislation. The book deals with the nation's forty years in the wilderness, the result of the people's fear and unbelief when God presented them with entering the Promised Land.

**Deuteronomy.** Moses' three discourses to the nation and his death are recorded in Deuteronomy. In his discourses, the great leader of Israel addressed Israel's past, present, and future. Moses appointed Joshua as the next leader of Israel and exhorted the people to be strong in the Lord (31). The book also contains Moses' song (32) and his blessings on the tribes (33). The final chapter traces Moses' journey up Mount Nebo in Moab where he died.

3. Read Deuteronomy 32:1–4. What did Moses so poetically conclude about God?

## The Books of History

The books of history cover a period of one thousand years—from 1447 BC to 432 BC. They start with the conquest of the Promised Land and end with the divided kingdoms of Israel and Judah. The historical books are mostly narrative accounts.

**Joshua.** The book of Joshua relates how Moses' successor, Joshua, led the nation in conquering and possessing the land of Canaan. The first victory was at Jericho. Ai was the place of defeat due to the sin and disobedience of a soldier named Achan. Joshua first struck through the center of the land, defeated the south, and finally the north. At Joshua's death, Israel was in the Promised Land with the majority of the land possessed and more conquering yet to complete.

**Judges.** Judges ruled the Promised Land during the time between Joshua and king Saul. The book of Judges describes their exploits. The judges functioned more like generals than judges of our day. During the three hundred years spanned by this book, Israel went through cycles, going from peace to apostasy to oppression to repentance to deliverance to peace. The book mentions twelve judges. It was a time when *every man did that which was right in his own eyes* (21:25). Thus, it has been labeled *the dark days of the judges*. The last five chapters describe the religious, social, and political confusion of the day.

**Ruth.** Ruth presents the bright side of the period of the judges. It describes God's grace through a remnant that feared Him. Ruth, a Moabitess, chose to worship the God of Israel and worked to provide for her Jewish widowed mother-in law, Naomi.

4. Ruth 1:16, 17. Describe the love Ruth showed for Naomi.

In time Ruth married Boaz and became an ancestress of David's and ultimately of Christ's.

**1 Samuel.** First Samuel concludes the account of the period of the judges and describes the founding of the Hebrew monarchy. The book starts with the judgeships of Eli and Samuel, describes the rise and fall of King Saul, and concludes with the rise of King David. Eli was a high priest with wicked sons. Samuel was a God-fearing leader who helped stabilize the nation while he was at its helm. Saul began as a humble man, but he allowed power to corrupt him, and he lost God's favor through disobedience. His life ended in defeat on the battlefield.

**2 Samuel, 1 Chronicles.** Second Samuel and 1 Chronicles essentially cover the same period of time. First Chronicles has ten chapters of genealogies that emphasize the theocratic lineage of David. Both 1 and 2 Chronicles were probably written after Judah's return from captivity, possibly by Ezra. Second Samuel and 1 Chronicles both deal with King David's reign. David was a great military leader and a godly man. He defeated all of Israel's enemies and enlarged the kingdom. However, he later fell into immorality with Bathsheba, the wife of Uriah. David repented, but during his last years he reaped the consequences of his sin.

**1 and 2 Kings, 2 Chronicles.** First and 2 Kings parallel 2 Chronicles. They begin with the reign of Solomon. Upon Solomon's death his kingdom split into the Southern Kingdom composed of Judah and Benjamin, and the Northern Kingdom that included the ten northern tribes. The split came as a judgment on Solomon for going after the gods of the many pagan wives he married. Eventually Assyria carried the northern tribes into captivity in 722 BC. The Southern Kingdom fell to Babylon in 586 BC. First and 2 Kings were written from a prophetic viewpoint. Second Chronicles was written from a priestly perspective.

**Ezra.** The book of Ezra is about the restoration of Judah and Jerusalem after the Babylonian captivity. The book has a break in the middle that spans fifty-eight years. The first half of the book (1–6) deals with the first return under Governor Zerubbabel and Joshua the high priest. The second half (7–10) covers the second return under Ezra. During the fifty-eight-year break, the events of the book of Esther took place.

**Nehemiah.** Nehemiah is a record of the incredible rebuilding of the walls of Jerusalem despite opposition and threat of attack. The last part deals with revival among the Jews under the leadership of both Ezra and Nehemiah.

**Esther.** God is not mentioned in the book of Esther. The providence of God, however, is clearly seen. This book describes the evil plot of Haman as he sought to destroy the Jews. God providentially thwarted Haman's plot through the efforts of Esther and Mordecai. The message of the book is that God protected His people even while they were in captivity. The message of God's providence and faithful care is strong.

## The Books of Poetry

The Bible contains six books of poetry. The primary characteristic of Biblical poetry is parallel structure, where two thoughts are placed in relationship to each other.

**Job.** Job describes the experience of a righteous man who suffered many hardships. He lost all of his possessions, his family, and his health. His three friends tried to convince him that his misfortunes were due to sin in his life, but Job maintained his innocence. The book contains much dialogue between Job and the three friends. In the end God vindicated Job and restored his prosperity once Job learned to

**Psalms.** Psalms is a collection of 150 songs. David wrote about half of them. Some of the other writers include Moses, Solomon, and Asaph. There are eight types of psalms, including hymns (113, 150), laments (42, 43), thanksgiving psalms (56, 100), psalms of confidence (11), psalms of remembrance (105), wisdom psalms (1, 12), kingship psalms (20, 93), and imprecatory psalms (10, 69).

Though written by and for Israelites and in a different dispensation with different worship practices, the psalms have universal appeal. Today we find the psalms to be a great source of comfort, worship, challenge, and encouragement.

5. What is your favorite psalm?

6. Why are the Psalms often comforting in times of trouble?

**Proverbs.** Proverbs contains many wise sayings, which are common bywords dealing with life on earth. Most of the proverbs were the work of Solomon addressed to his son, Rehoboam. They still provide great wisdom for young people today. A theme of Proverbs is, *The fear of the Lord is the beginning of knowledge* (Prov. 1:7).

**Ecclesiastes.** Solomon also wrote Ecclesiastes, which looks at life through the eyes of a natural man who finds no pleasure or purpose in life. The natural man concludes that all is *vanity and vexation of spirit* (1:14; 2:11; 6:9). In the book's conclusion, Solomon challenged the reader to *remember now thy Creator in the days of thy youth* (12:1) and to *fear God, and keep his commandments* (12:13).

**Song of Solomon.** The final book by Solomon is the Song of Solomon. It is a love song describing the love of a bridegroom and his bride. The song honors marriage and wedded love. As part of God's inspired Word, it is more than a secular book on love; it is human love from God's perspective.

**Lamentations.** The prophet Jeremiah wrote the book of Lamentations. Jeremiah prophesied the fall of Jerusalem to Babylon (Jer. 1:14–16). After the city fell, he wrote Lamentations. Yet in this book of sorrows, Jeremiah recorded the promise of God's faithfulness (Lam. 3:31, 32).

## Major Prophets

Sixteen prophetic books make up the last section of the Old Testament. The terms *Major Prophets* and *Minor Prophets* refer to the lengths of the books.

7. What comes to your mind when you think of the Old Testament books of prophecy?

8. Name one truth you learned about God from reading or studying the prophets.

The prophets ministered from the times of the kings to the days after the return from exile. The prophets' writings are some of the most dramatic and descriptive in all of Scripture. They communicate on both an intellectual and an emotional level so that God's heart is both understood and felt. Quality time spent in the prophets will cause lasting change in one's relationship with God.

**Isaiah.** Isaiah is often called the *prophet of the Messiah* since he had more to say about the Messiah than any other prophet did. Also he is called the *evangelical prophet* because of chapter 53, which is the clearest presentation of the gospel in the Old Testament. With sixty-six chapters, Isaiah has more chapters than any Old Testament book, except Psalms.

**Jeremiah.** The *weeping prophet* is the name often used for Jeremiah. He wept for his fellow Israelites and gave more biography on Israel than any other prophet. He received his call from God when he was a youth (1:6), and proclaimed that the Jews should surrender to Babylon. Because of his message, Jeremiah was one of Judah's most unpopular prophets. The Jewish leaders made several attempts on his life; they threw him into a cistern, put him in stocks, and later imprisoned him. Nevertheless, Jeremiah remained true to God in spite of all his sufferings.

**Ezekiel.** The Babylonians carried Ezekiel away into captivity when he was a young man. He saw many visions, such as the wheel in the middle of a wheel and the valley of dry bones. He was known to act out his messages; e.g., digging a hole in the wall and lying on his side for many days. His prophecies served to communicate God's love and grace to the needy captives in a highly visual way.

**Daniel.** The Babylonians also took into captivity Daniel and his three friends. The first part of Daniel's book gives historical events of his life, such as his ordeal in the lions' den. The second part describes prophecies of the future concerning Israel and the Gentile nations.

## Minor Prophets

**Hosea.** Hosea is often called the *prophet of divine love.*

9. Read Hosea 1:2. Is this how you would imagine a book about divine love would start? Explain.

Hosea fell in love with Gomer and married her, but she was unfaithful to him. Eventually she became a prostitute and ended up a slave for sale in the slave market. Hosea still loved her, bought her, and brought her home. His love is a picture of God's love for Israel. As such, Hosea is a powerfully touching book that leaves the reader with an awe of God's love.

**Joel.** *Jehovah is God* is the meaning of Joel's name. He began his book by referring to a locust plague which devastated the land (1:4). He also called for mourning because and the grapevines and fruit trees were withered (1:12). This set the stage for his prophecy concerning *the Day of the Lord* (1:15), a time of judgment from God. The Tribulation will be *a day of darkness and of gloominess, a day of clouds and of thick darkness* (2:2). Therefore, the nation was to repent and turn to the Lord with all its heart (2:12). Joel ended his prophecy with the blessing and restoration of God's people.

**Amos.** Amos was a herdsman and a gatherer of sycamore fruit who was called by God (7:14). Many times he used the phrase *for three transgressions . . . and for four* (1:3, 6), depicting sin multiplied upon sin. He pronounced judgment on many neighboring nations and zeroed in on Israel, the Northern Kingdom. Amos received a number of visions: locusts, fire, the plumb line, and the basket of summer fruit (7; 8). These visions foretold coming judgment.

**Obadiah.** The book of Obadiah is the shortest book of the Old Testament and is not divided into chapters. Obadiah prophesied against Edom, the descendants of Esau, who lived in red rock cliffs surrounding Petra. He warned these descendants that God would judge Edom for its animosity toward its *brother* Judah (12–15).

**Jonah.** God called Jonah to preach against Nineveh, the capital of Assyria. It was the cruelest of all the ancient nations, and its wickedness came up before God (1:2). At first Jonah refused to go to Ninevah and tried to flee to Tarshish, but God stopped him with a storm and a big fish. After God delivered Jonah, the prophet went to Nineveh. He was not happy, however, when the city repented and God spared it from destruction. In the end God pointed out the error of Jonah's ways through an object lesson involving a withered plant.

**Micah.** The book of Micah begins with a vivid description of the holiness of God.

10. Read Micah 1:3, 4. How does the descriptive language help you understand the holiness of God?

Micah used many Hebrew puns to prophesy coming judgment on Judah. Micah was a social reformer who was concerned about his country. He spoke out against the rich, who were taking fields and houses from the poor and were oppressing them (2:2), and the prophets, priests, and judges, who were all corrupt (2; 3). Micah also prophesied that in the latter days, Jerusalem would be the center of worship for all nations (4). Micah is also noted for his prophecy of Christ's birth in Bethlehem (5:2).

**Nahum.** The book opens with a description of God: God is jealous for His people and will not acquit the wicked (1:2). God used Assyria to judge the Northern Kingdom, but Assyria was ruthless in how it conquered and treated the captives. Nahum predicted the fall of Nineveh, the capital of Assyria. God's judgment on Assyria would be great and total (3:19). This prophecy was fulfilled in 612 BC.

**Habakkuk.** In his prophetic book, Habakkuk described a debate he had with God. Habakkuk's first concern was why God did not judge Judah for its sin (1:1—2:1). God stated that He was going to judge Judah by letting it fall into the hands of Babylon (2:1–20). Habakkuk could not understand how God could do this since Babylon was more wicked than Judah, but God also promised to punish Babylon (3).

**Zephaniah.** Like Joel, Zephaniah prophesied the coming *day of the Lord*. Zephaniah gives a vivid description of the tribulation period. It will be a day of wrath, trouble, devastation, desolation, darkness, gloominess, clouds, and thick darkness (1:15). Through the Tribulation God will purify Israel and then regather His people (3:20).

**Haggai.** The prophet Haggai rose up to provoke the Jews who had returned from the Babylonian captivity to rebuild the temple, the Lord's house. They had laid the foundation but then grew apathetic toward spiritual things, caring more about their own houses than about the house of the Lord (1:4–8).

11. Read Haggai 1:3–5. Describe the tone of the Lord's message through Haggai.

Haggai challenged the remnant to be faithful and promised them that God would guarantee their peace and the prosperity of Jerusalem (2:3–5).

**Zechariah.** The prophet Zechariah was a contemporary with Haggai. He preached repentance and then recorded prophecies concerning the coming Messiah and end-time events (1:7—6:8). He saw visions of horses, four chariots, horns, a measuring line, Joshua (the high priest), a branch, a lamp stand and olive trees, a flying scroll, and a woman in a basket. The book ends with prophecies about the Messiah's coming, His rejection, and eventual kingdom (9—14).

**Malachi.** Malachi was concerned about the lack of genuine worship within Israel. The nation was going through the motions of worship, but it was all ritual and not from the heart. The priests were corrupt (2:1–4), and husbands were unfaithful to their wives (2:14). Malachi pointed out that God hates divorce (2:16). Malachi predicted the coming of John the Baptist who would prepare the way of the Lord at His first coming to earth (3:1).

## MAKING IT PERSONAL

12. Which parts of the Old Testament are you most familiar with?

13. What has contributed to that familiarity?

14. What books in the Old Testament do you want to become more familiar with?

15. What steps will you take to become more familiar with those books?

# New Testament Books



## Scripture Focus

Various Bible passage

## Theme

God inspired each book of the New Testament with purpose and for our benefit.

**Memory Verse**

*"Behold, I come quickly: blessed is he that keepeth the sayings of the prophecy of this book" (Revelation 22:7).*

## GETTING STARTED

The older we get the blurrier our memories are about which sibling or child did what. Was it Bob or Ted who pulled the cat's tail? Was it Lizzy or Sara who stepped in front of a swing and got knocked out cold?

1. Have you ever become confused about which sibling or child said or did something in the past?

2. How would you describe each one of your children (or siblings)?

The New Testament books are like two families. There are the four Gospels and there are all the Epistles. It is easy to get them confused and forget which Gospel and which Epistle says what. This lesson will give an overview of each of the books and challenge you to get to know some of the New Testament books a little better.

## SEARCHING THE SCRIPTURES

The New Testament is a collection of twenty-seven writings composed over a period of about fifty years by less than ten different writers. The writers were either apostles or companions of apostles. The New Testament contains various *genres*, or types, of literature. For example, the Gospels are most like ancient biographies, the book of Acts is a history, the Epistles are letters, and the book of Revelation is an apocalyptic work.

### Gospels and Acts

The New Testament contains four books classified as the Gospels. The word *gospel* means *good news*, and these books relate the good news about Jesus Christ. The first three are known as the synoptic Gospels, since they share a similar structure and similar materials. All three synoptic Gospels discuss Jesus' Galilean ministry, then His journey south to Judea, and finally His ministry and last days in Jerusalem. The fourth Gospel, the book of John, describes Jesus' ministry journeys back and forth between Galilee and Judea, and it contains many unique episodes in Jesus' life.

**Matthew.** Matthew makes a fitting bridge between the Old Testament and the rest of the New Testament since it stresses the Jewish character of Jesus. The book of Matthew emphasizes Christ's fulfillment of the Old Testament Scriptures, and the opening genealogy shows Jesus' position as a descendant of Abraham. Matthew's Gospel portrays Jesus as King and repeatedly refers to *the kingdom of heaven* (3:2, 8:11, 13:24). Matthew includes important lengthy teachings of Jesus, such as the Sermon on the Mount (5—7). The Gospel accentuates the concept of righteousness, and Jesus' authority is contrasted with that of the hypocritical religious leaders.

**Mark.** Mark was written by John Mark, a companion of Paul and later Peter. Unlike Matthew and Luke, which begin with Jesus' infancy, this Gospel immediately begins with Jesus' adult ministry. Mark highlighted Jesus' activity more than His teachings and depicted Jesus as the obedient servant.

3. Read Mark 10:45. How does Mark describe Jesus' ministry?

Mark emphasizes the final sufferings of Jesus, and almost one-third of the book describes the last week of Jesus' life.

**Luke.** Luke was a companion of Paul and wrote both the Gospel of Luke and the book of Acts. The book of Luke portrays Jesus as the Savior both of Jews and Gentiles.

4. Read Luke 19:10. How did Luke portray Jesus' ministry?

Luke's Gospel also stresses Jesus' interest in the poor, the role of the Holy Spirit, and the importance of prayer. The book contains several famous parables, such as the parable of the Good Samaritan (10) and the parables of the lost sheep, the lost coin, and the Prodigal Son (15).

**John.** The Gospel of John was written by the apostle John, who appears in the narrative as the anonymous *beloved disciple* (13:23; 19:26, 27).

5. Read John 20:31. What was John's stated purpose for his Gospel?

John describes Jesus' miracles as *signs* of His true identity as God the Son, the Word, Who came into the world (1:1, 14; 20:28). Belief is the proper response to Jesus, since He is one with the Father. When one believes, he or she is *born again* and receives new life (3:3). The book also contains Jesus' seven *I am* statements: *I am the bread of life* (6:35); *I am the light of the world* (8:12); *I am the door* (10:7); *I am the good shepherd* (10:11); *I am the resurrection and the life* (11:25); *I am the way, the truth, and the life* (14:6); and *I am the true vine* (15:1). John's Gospel is the only one to rehearse such events as the wedding at Cana (2), the conversation with Nicodemus (3), the conversation with the Samaritan woman at the well (4), the raising of Lazarus (11), and the washing of the disciples' feet (13). John also contains the Upper Room Discourse, in which Jesus promised to send the Holy Spirit (13—17). Like all the other Gospels, John ends with the crucifixion and resurrection of Jesus (18—21).

**Acts.** The book of Acts describes the birth and early growth of the church. Luke, the writer, appears within the narrative in the *we* sections.

The early chapters recount the Holy Spirit's coming with power at Pentecost. After being empowered with the Holy Spirit, believers were to become witnesses *in Jerusalem, and in all Judaea, and in Samaria, and unto the uttermost part of the earth* (1:8). The early chapters depict the Jerusalem church under the leadership of Peter and James, the half-brother of Jesus. The second half of the book focuses on the ministry of the apostle Paul. Paul took three missionary journeys in what is now Turkey and Greece. After he was arrested, he was taken to Rome as a prisoner.

## The Pauline Epistles

The apostle Paul wrote more New Testament books than any other writer. His collection of letters is called the Pauline Epistles.

**Galatians.** The book of Galatians offers the reader a good introduction to Paul's teaching on theology in the areas of justification by faith alone, freedom in Christ, and life in the Spirit. The Galatians had been troubled by false teachers who attempted to bring them under the law and imposed circumcision for the sake of acceptance with God.

6. Read Galatians 1:6–9. What did Paul instruct concerning the gospel preached by false teachers?

**Romans.** Romans, the most systematic of Paul's epistles, discusses many of the same issues as Galatians. Romans describes God's righteousness as it is demonstrated in the gospel (1:17). Every human, both Jew and Gentile, is a sinner and is justly under God's wrath (1—3). But God justifies, or declares righteous, those who place their faith in Christ (4; 5). God's grace is not a license to sin, however, since the Holy Spirit has been given to enable the believer to live a holy life (6—8). Although it seems that God has set aside Israel in His plan of salvation, He has neither completely nor finally cast them off (9—11). A believing remnant survives, and in the future Israel will again experience spiritual blessing (11:26). The end of Romans concerns Christian living in relation to service (12), government (13), and those with differing convictions (14).

**1 and 2 Corinthians.** The New Testament includes two of Paul's letters to the church in Corinth. First Corinthians deals with a catalog of problems in the church. The Corinthian assembly suffered from disunity, immaturity, sexual immorality, lawsuits, questions about marriage, the issue of food sacrificed to idols, a lack of church decorum, and abuse of the Lord's Supper. Chapters 12 through 14 concern the nature and use of spiritual gifts, including the essential role of love (13). All things are to *be done decently and in order* (14:40). Chapter 15 is a lengthy discussion of the doctrine of the Resurrection.

Second Corinthians is a defense of Paul's ministry. Even in weakness, Paul boasted in the Lord Jesus and His grace and power (2 Cor. 4:5; 12:9). Paul encouraged his readers to be ambassadors for God's ministry of reconciliation (5), and he discussed principles of Christian stewardship (8; 9).

**1 and 2 Thessalonians.** First and 2 Thessalonians were written to Paul's church plant in Thessalonica, the capital of Macedonia. The two epistles primarily concern future events, since the church was troubled by various misunderstandings. Evidently, some of the Thessalonian believers were worried that their Christian loved ones who had died would miss the Lord's return.

7. Read 1 Thess. 4:13–18. What truths did Paul spell out for the Thessalonians?

In the meantime, the Thessalonians were to *watch and be sober* (5:6). They were to wait for the *Son from heaven . . . even Jesus, which delivered us from the wrath to come* (1:10).

In the case of 2 Thessalonians, it seems that church members were afraid that the Day of Christ had come (2 Thess. 2:2), but Paul assured them it had not yet arrived. The Thessalonians were to continue working while they waited for Christ with expectancy (3:6–12). They were commanded to *stand fast, and hold the traditions which ye have been taught* (2:15). Christ would come again to Earth and take vengeance on His enemies (1:7–10).

**Ephesians and Colossians.** Colossae was located near Ephesus in what is modern-day Turkey. Both Colossians and Ephesians depict the relationship between Christ and His Body, the church (Eph. 1:22, 23; Col. 1:18). Both describe putting off the old man and putting on the new man (Eph. 4:22–24; Col. 3:9, 10). Both also exhort various household members to fulfill their rightful duties (Eph. 5:22—6:9; Col. 3:18—4:1). Ephesians emphasizes the *walk* of the believer (Eph. 2:2, 10; 4:1, 17; 5:2, 8, 15). The letter also relates the believer's election to spiritual blessings in Christ (1) and details the Christian's spiritual armor (6). Some type of heresy had influenced the church in Colossae. The Colossians were tempted to worship angels, and so Paul accentuated the preeminence of Christ (Col. 2:18, 19).

**Philemon.** At the same time that Paul composed Colossians, he also wrote Philemon. Paul was writing on behalf of Onesimus, a slave who had run away from his owner, Philemon, and had later converted to Christ. Paul petitioned Philemon to receive Onesimus back no longer as a slave, but as a beloved brother (16). The apostle offered to pay any debt incurred by Onesimus (18, 19).

**Philippians.** The final Prison Epistle is Philippians, written to the church at Philippi in Macedonia. In this book Paul highlighted unity in purpose and love (1:27—2:2), joy and rejoicing (4:4), and humility (2:3, 4). In a beautifully poetic passage, Paul exalted Jesus as an example of humble service (2:5–11).

8. Read Philippians 1:21. What was Paul's personal testimony regarding his purpose in life?

**1 Timothy.** First Timothy refers to Timothy as Paul's *son in the faith* (1:2). Paul encouraged Timothy to be exemplary in his character and conduct (4:12). Along with this encouragement, Paul described proper prayer and worship (2), outlined the requirements for church offices (3), and gave an overview of church administration (5).

**2 Timothy.** In 2 Timothy the apostle seemed to anticipate an impending martyrdom (4:6). Paul commanded Timothy to pass on the faith to the next generation and to disciple others (2:2). Timothy was to be diligent in his personal life, to preach the Word, and to *reprove, rebuke, exhort with all longsuffering and doctrine* (4:2).

9. Read 2 Timothy 4:1–4. Why was Timothy to be careful to preach the Word?

**Titus.** Titus was Paul's *son after the common faith* (1:4). Paul's letter to him stressed the need for sound doctrine (1:3; 2:5, 10) and emphasized God's love, mercy, and grace (3:4–7).

## The General Epistles and Revelation

The next grouping in the New Testament is the General Epistles, which were written by several different men to various audiences.

**Hebrews.** Hebrews is the largest General Epistle. While some Bible teachers believe that the apostle Paul wrote Hebrews, no writer's name is mentioned in the text itself; therefore, the writer's identity has been debated. The writer described his work as a *word of exhortation*, a phrase sometimes used of sermons (13:22; cf. Acts 13:15). Hebrews exhorts its readers toward spiritual maturity (Heb. 5:11—6:1) and warns against neglect, unbelief, and apostasy. The book of Hebrews also offers doctrinal truths about Jesus Christ: He is superior to angels, Old Testament leaders, and Jewish ceremonies. As both High Priest (4:14, 15) and perfect sacrifice (10:11–14), Jesus is better than the Old Testament sacrificial system.

**James.** The book of James offers practical counsel on living out one's faith in everyday life. Faith outwardly demonstrates itself in action (2:14–26). The writer James described impartiality (2), godly speech (3), submission to God and the proper use of riches (4; 5), patience and prayer (5), and wisdom and endurance in suffering (1).

10. Read James 1:22. What important point did James make concerning the Word?

**1 Peter.** First Peter deals with endurance in suffering. The words *suffer* and *suffering* appear fifteen times in this short letter, but Peter also highlighted the believer's future glory (1:7; 4:13; 5:10, 11). Thus Peter expounded a confident hope in the face of trials (1:3, 13, 21; 3:15). According to Peter, the very hardships Christians face can become opportunities for witness (3:13–17).

**2 Peter.** The subject matter of 2 Peter concentrates on false teachers. Second Peter warns of the final judgment upon false teachers (2), but it also reaffirms the second coming of Christ (3). Until Christ's return, the readers were to *be diligent* and to *grow in grace, and in the knowledge of our Lord and Saviour Jesus Christ* (3:14, 18).

**Jude.** The short epistle of Jude also opposes false teachers and uses many of the same Old Testament illustrations of judgment as 2 Peter. The ungodly opponents had departed from the faith and had espoused immoral lifestyles (4). Therefore, Jude exhorted his readers to *earnestly contend for the faith which was once delivered unto the saints* (3).

**1, 2, 3 John.** The apostle John wrote three General Epistles, probably around 90 AD. First John shares many of the same key words as his Gospel, such as *believe, life, light,* and *love.* First John was written because of the presence in the church of some apostates (1 John 2:18, 19). These false teachers denied that Jesus Christ came in the flesh (4:2, 3). Because of this false teaching, John highlighted the importance of fellowship, the vital relationship between God and His children (1:3–7). John also wrote to those who remained in the church that *ye may know that ye have eternal life* (5:13). The believers' relationship with God was demonstrated in their love for one another and in their sound doctrine. Second John stresses the need for *walking in truth* because *many deceivers are entered into the world* (2 John 4, 7). Third John commends Christian hospitality and condemns a love of preeminence.

**Revelation.** John also wrote the book of Revelation. Revelation was written to seven churches in Asia Minor (2; 3). Like other apocalyptic literature, the book of Revelation recounts various angelic activities and vivid, symbolic visions (cf. Dan. 7—12). The bulk of Revelation describes the tribulation period when God's wrath will be poured out upon the inhabitants of the world (Rev. 4—19). God's judgments are arranged by seven seals, seven trumpets, and seven bowls. Interspersed within these judgments are descriptions of major tribulation characters such as the Antichrist, the false prophet, the two faithful witnesses, and the 144,000 Jews. At the end of the Tribulation, the Lamb (Christ) will return to conquer His enemies at the Battle of Armageddon (19). He will bind Satan and rule for 1,000 years (20). Following one final battle, Christ will judge all unbelievers at the Great White Throne Judgment (20). Believers, on the other hand, will enjoy the glories of the New Jerusalem (21).

11. Read Revelation 21:4. How does John describe life in eternity?

## MAKING IT PERSONAL

12. Which parts of the New Testament would you say you know well?

13. What has contributed to that knowledge?

14. What books in the New Testament do you want to learn more about?

15. What steps will you take to learn more about those books?

# To the Praise of His Glory

LESSON 12

## Scripture Focus

Gen. 1; Exod. 3:14; 15; 24:16–18; Num. 14:20–24; 20:12; Ps. 19:1–6; Isa. 40; Matt. 17:1–5; John 1:14; Eph. 1:3–14; 5:8–21; Rev. 21:9–23

## Theme

God's overarching purpose is to bring glory to His name.

**Memory Verses**

*"And I saw no temple therein: for the Lord God Almighty and the Lamb are the temple of it. And the city had no need of the sun, neither of the moon, to shine in it: for the glory of God did lighten it, and the Lamb is the light thereof" (Revelation 21:22, 23).*

## GETTING STARTED

Color is essentially light. That becomes obvious when we observe raindrops refracting light to form a rainbow. In fact, we would not have color without light. And we could not see color without the cones in our eyes. People with rod vision see everything in grayscale.

1. What might the refraction of light have to do with the glory of God?

2. What might life be like if we could not see colors?

When God made light, He essentially made color. To this day His creation causes us to stand in awe as we observe its beautiful color combinations. The abundance of color in creation should cause us to glorify God. When we do, we are fulfilling His purpose for His creation in the first place.

This lesson is about God's overarching purpose that He reveals to us in His Word. We will see that beginning with the creation of light in Genesis to the presence of His light in Revelation, God's main focus has always been His glory.

## SEARCHING THE SCRIPTURES

God's glory is the manifestation of all that is true about God. When He reveals His glory, He is essentially revealing truth about His character and ways. Bringing glory to God, then, is reflecting or declaring His glorious character and ways so that others might see them and learn about God. Bringing glory to God is telling or demonstrating Who God is.

### God Created for His Glory

God began the six days of creation by creating light (Gen. 1:3). Later, on day four, He created the sun, moon, stars, and various other heavenly bodies that would produce and reflect the light we see in the heavens today (1:14). Why did God begin with light and then wait three days to give that light a physical source? Because God is the original source of light. He is light. No other light is needed besides Him. Yet He chose to put sources of light in the heavens as a testimony to the light in Him.

Psalm 19:1–6 relates God's creation of the heavens to the revelation of His glory. The heavens are filled with an unmeasurable amount of stars, planets, moons, comets, asteroids, quasars, and other yet to be identified objects. The massive size of the things of space, their mindboggling quantities, and the unfathomable expanse of space itself declares God's power and deity loud and clear (Rom. 1:20).

3. Read Psalm 19:1–6. What part does the sun play in declaring the glory of God?

That the heavens declare God's glory is not by accident. God created the heavens and the rest of nature, including humanity, for the express purpose of declaring His glory.

4. Read Isaiah 6:1–3. What do the seraphim around the throne of God declare concerning God's glory?

The fact that creation declares God's glory is not a coincidence. Rather it is a testimony to God's forethought and desire for humanity to know Him. Of course we have to realize that we now live on a cursed earth. What God's original creation in the pre-Fall days was able to communicate to humanity was better in some ways than what His creation is able to reveal today. But that God created for His glory is unmistakable.

## God Chose Israel for His Glory

Once Adam sinned, the world changed and humanity's relationship with God was broken. Eventually nearly the entire world's population refused to glorify God. God then destroyed them all, sparing only Noah's family. Noah's ark is a demonstration of God's glorious grace (Gen. 6:8).

After Noah, there was little acknowledgment of God as creator and nearly no recognition of the need for forgiveness of sin. God then called Abraham to follow Him. Abraham responded to God by faith. God made a covenant with Abraham, promising posterity, land, and blessing for all the earth (Gen. 12:1–3; 15:18).

Centuries later God chose Moses to lead His people out of Egypt. God came to Moses as *I AM THAT I AM* (Exod. 3:14), a name that captures God's self-existence. God then went on to reveal Himself as the *I AM* to the people of Israel as they left Egypt and crossed the Red Sea. After God drowned the Egyptian army in the Red Sea, Moses wrote a song about the revelation of God's glory.

5. Read Exodus 15:1–10. What did God make known about Himself by delivering Israel through the Red Sea (v. 6)?

6. Read Exodus 15:11–13. What else did the Red Sea crossing reveal about God (v. 11)?

The Red Sea crossing established the fact of God's power and character with both the children of Israel and the Canaanites in the Promised Land (Exod. 15:14–19). God *triumphed gloriously* in delivering His people from Egypt (15:20, 21). But His plans to use Israel to reveal His glory were only beginning.

God led His people to Mount Sinai where His glory rested on the mountain as a *devouring fire* (Exod. 24:16–18). The message to the people was that God is holy and demands holiness from His people. The people, being stubborn and inclined to do their own thing, disobeyed God by creating and worshiping a gold calf (32:1–6). Moses pleaded with God not to destroy His people. When God promised not to destroy them, Moses asked God to show him His glory (33:18). God did so in grand fashion.

7. Read Exodus 34:5–7. What did God reveal about Himself to Moses?

As Israel's leader, Moses understood that the journey to the Promised Land was not simply about reaching a destination; it was about glorifying God along the way and eventually in the Promised Land.

Israel continued to make their way to the doorstep of the Promised Land. When they arrived, they feared the giant inhabitants and refused to enter the land. God judged them severely, condemning all those twenty years old and older to die in the wilderness within a forty-year period.

8. Read Numbers 14:20–24. What was God's purpose for giving Israel the Promised Land?

God's punishment of Israel was so serious because they robbed Him of His glory. How small God must have looked to the Egyptians and Canaanites as His people meandered through the wilderness for forty years. What a poor testimony to their great God.

Years after Israel finally entered the Promised Land, Israel was divided into two kingdoms, both of which were eventually taken into captivity because of their disobedience to God. Beginning in Isaiah 40, Isaiah prophesied concerning the captives of Judah in the land of Babylon. Isaiah anticipated the nation's captivity and her restoration seventy years later, and he wrote to encourage the people of Judah in their walk with God.

9. Read Isaiah 40:5. What did Isaiah prophesy would happen?

Centuries later Isaiah's prophecy was partially fulfilled in the coming of Christ. The ultimate fulfillment still awaits Christ's return to set up His millennial Kingdom. Isaiah's prophecy shows that even when the Israelites were languishing as captives in Babylon, God still talked of His plan to reveal His glory to all flesh.

10. Read Isaiah 40:6, 7. How sure is God's word concerning His plans to reveal His glory to all flesh?

Isaiah cried out concerning God's sure word so the captives in Babylon would have hope in their future as a nation. The message to us is that God took the revelation of His glory seriously. It was so important that He wanted Isaiah to shout about the message (40:6).

## God Sent Christ for His Glory

The Babylonian captivity was eventually ended and a remnant of God's people returned to Israel to rebuild Jerusalem. Over five centuries later, God sent His Son into the world. In his Gospel, John wrote about the arrival of Jesus, the *Word*. He wrote that Jesus had given *life* as the creator and in Him was God's *light* (John 1:4). So Jesus gave *physical* light at the creation of the world and then gave *spiritual* light at His coming to earth. In giving spiritual light, Jesus revealed the truth about Himself and the Father. That truth shows humanity their need for a Savior and that Jesus is the One Whom the Father sent to save them. Jesus' revelation of the truth about salvation means that there is also *eternal* life in Jesus.

11. Read John 1:1–5, 14. What did John say Jesus revealed?

As the world watched Jesus, they got a glimpse of God's glory. His words and actions made God's glory visible to them. Jesus was a testimony to what God is like. Ultimately Jesus' humble death on the cross revealed God's love and grace.

As mentioned above, Christ's ultimate glory will be seen in the millennial Kingdom. Jesus' transfiguration, witnessed by Peter, James, and John, was a preview of the glory He will reveal in His future kingdom (Matt. 16:28—17:9; 2 Pet. 1:16–18). Christ's glory at His transfiguration was evident as a bright light. Matthew's description is that Christ's face shone *as the sun* (Matt. 17:2). That comparison harkens back to the creation of light on the first day of creation and the dependence on God's light until the sun was created on the fourth day.

The apostle Paul wrote about the connection between Christ's mission to bring salvation and the glory of God.

12. Read Ephesians 1:3–6. Why did Jesus choose us before the foundation of the world and predestinate us to the adoption as His sons?

13. Read Ephesians 1:7–12. Why did God redeem and forgive us (v. 12)?

14. Read Ephesians 1:13, 14. Why did God seal us by His Spirit until the day of redemption?

Paul leaves no doubt that God's ultimate purpose in choosing us, redeeming us, and sealing us was that we might praise His glory. When we consider the blessings of salvation, praising God's glorious grace is a no-brainer.

*Redemption* denotes a release from slavery by paying a ransom. Christ paid a ransom to deliver us from the bondage and consequences of sin (Mark 10:45). *Redeem* means to loose from something. Before we trusted in Christ, we were slaves to sin. However, when Christ redeemed us by His blood, He emancipated us from our slavery to sin. That is worth praising God every day of our lives.

The means of redeeming us from sin was Christ's blood (Eph. 1:7b). The apostle John wrote: *The blood of Jesus Christ his [God's] Son cleanseth us from all sin* (1 John 1:7b). Paul explained the practical meaning of redemption by assuring the Ephesians—and us—that Christ's redemptive work provided the *forgiveness of sins* (Eph. 1:7c). Although redemption includes more than forgiveness, forgiveness is basic to its meaning.

## God Commissioned the Church for His Glory

Salvation is just the beginning of God's plan to glorify His name through us. His will is for the church to bring glory to His name throughout this present age. He has commissioned us to make disciples, teaching them all that He commanded us to do (Matt. 28:18–20). The disciple-making process will lead to God being glorified.

Paul addressed what it means to live as a disciple that is pleasing to God (Eph. 5:1–21). He commanded the believers at Ephesus to be imitators of God by walking in *love* and in the *light* (5:1, 8). To *walk as children of light* is to reflect God's glory. It is to live as Christ would. This is possible because of the power of the Holy Spirit to produce *goodness*, *righteousness*, and *truth* in us (5:9, 18). *Goodness* is showing love to others. *Righteousness* refers to our character from God's perspective. Other people will see our righteous character in our actions. *Truth* is genuineness. It speaks of pure motives and honesty.

As we walk in the light as disciples of Christ, we will be in stark contrast to the darkness around us. Paul told the Ephesians to *reprove* the *unfruitful works of darkness* (5:11). God's light, or His glory, in our lives will shine into the lives of the lost and help them see their need for a Savior. This process of exposing *unfruitful works of darkness* is actually what God expects of us (5:12, 13). We really don't have an option to not walk in the light.

15. Read Ephesians 5:14. What did God tell the Ephesian believers to do?

The word *circumspectly* in verse 15 means to *look around*. Paul told the *drowsy* Ephesians to be aware of what is really happening around them. We too need to take time to look around us and consider how things really are. The world desperately needs to see the light of the truth in our lives. They need a glimpse of God's glory. Shining God's glory through our lives shows wisdom. Wisdom is seeing life from God's perspective and responding accordingly. Ignoring reality is foolish (5:15).

Our time to walk in the light and introduce the lost to the reality of Christ is limited. Paul instructed the Ephesians to *redeem*, or *buy up*, their time on earth (5:16, 17). *Time* refers to a critical period of time or a special opportunity. Every believer's life is critical to the cause of Christ.

Paul summarized his instructions in Ephesians in one verse in his letter to Corinth.

16. Read 1 Corinthians 10:31. What one statement summarizes Paul's instructions to the Ephesians?

Walking in the light is to reflect God's glory. We should strive to make God's glory known through our lives every day (Phil. 1:21; 3:17–21).

## God Consummates All Things for His Glory

The Bible begins with the glory of God Illuminating God's creation for three days. It ends with the glory of God again providing illumination in eternity. When God consummates all things, His glory will be our focus forever.

17. Revelation 21:9–11a. How does John first describe the New Jerusalem (v. 11a)?

18. Read Revelation 21:11b–21. What part does light and color play in the New Jerusalem?

The New Jerusalem on the new earth will be a sight this earth has never or will ever know. Its brilliance and colors will reflect God's glory forever on the new earth. In fact, the new earth will have neither a sun nor a moon. God's glory will illuminate it forever (Rev. 21:22, 23). There won't be dark places or even shadows on the new earth.

The consummation of all things will be wonderful as the glory of God shines brightly forever. God's purpose to glorify His name will be fully realized. Until then, we ought to heed His Word and be about His business of glorifying His name through our lives today.

## MAKING IT PERSONAL

19. Has bringing glory to God been a goal for your life? Explain.

20. What have you done recently to bring glory to God?

21. How will you let God's glory impact your life going forward?

# Equipped to Serve

LESSON 13

## Scripture Focus

John 13:3–17; 2 Cor. 5:9, 10; Eph. 2:10; 2 Tim. 3:17;
Heb. 4:12, 13; 1 Pet. 2:2; 3:9–15

## Theme

God equips us to do good works through His Word.

**Memory Verse**

*"For we are his workmanship, created in Christ Jesus unto good works, which God hath before ordained that we should walk in them" (Ephesians 2:10).*

## GETTING STARTED

When a person wears the same cologne or perfume consistently over a long period of time, the fragrance becomes part of who he or she is. Just smelling the fragrance causes others to think of that person.

1. What fragrance, if any, have you worn consistently over an extended period of time?

2. What are some fragrances you identify with a spouse, parent, or friend?

Being in the Bible will have a lasting effect on believers. Others will identify them as having been in the Word. It will become the *fragrance* of their lives. This study is about being in the Word that it might affect your life.

God's Word prepares the hearts and minds of believers for service. This fact is not a coincidence but part of God's plan. God intends for believers to serve Him faithfully. As they do, they will bring glory to God.

After our relationship with God is established through trusting His Son for eternal life, we learn from our Lord and grow to be like Him through His Word. The Christian life is a life of good works. Scripture gives us clear reasons to pursue good works.

## Work to Fulfill Your Purpose

God's Word thoroughly furnishes us for all good works (2 Tim. 3:17). The words *throughly* and *all* are emphatic, not redundant. God has saved us to do good works, and He has spared nothing in making them possible. Second Timothy 3:17 should build our confidence as we consider the completeness of God's provision for us. It also should motivate us to study the Word so we will be ready to serve.

Many religious people believe that the purpose of good works is to secure salvation. This widely held error is obviously not Biblical. Yet if believers aren't careful, they can react so negatively against the teachings of works-salvation that they forget the integral part that works play in their lives. In a sense, the efforts of those trying to earn salvation are understandable. It is hard to accept that God would give eternal life as a gift to sinful people without requiring them to clean up their lives first.

3. Read Romans 5:6–8. For what types of persons was Christ willing to die?

4. What would characterize the type of person for whom you would be willing to die?

*Surely*, people might say, *with all the good I have done, I must have evened up the scales at least a little bit*. But no matter how good the intentions of those trying to earn salvation are, salvation is still only by grace through faith (Eph. 2:8, 9). We need to have our sin removed, not have it balanced by good works. God's grace brings us to the Cross, though our needs are many.

5. Read Ephesians 2:1–4. How do these verses describe the desperate needs of an unsaved person?

Unless God intervened, we would have no hope. His great love caused Him to show mercy to us (2:4). God did not give us the eternal punishment we deserved. Instead, as we trusted His provision for us in Christ, He gave us eternal life.

Though we work our hardest, not even our best could qualify us for salvation. It does not even make sense to think that we could do good works to qualify for eternal life. Paul asserted, *I do not frustrate the grace of God: for if righteousness come by the law, then Christ is dead in vain!* (Gal. 2:21). There really is no need for the Cross if we could work our way to Heaven.

Even though good works are not a part of securing salvation, they are an essential product of salvation. We should not take a lax approach to good works and view them as if they don't matter.

6. Read Ephesians 2:10. How does this verse underscore the importance of good works in the life of a believer?

The word *workmanship* means a *manufactured product*. It refers to God's work in us to prepare us to serve Him so we might fulfill our purpose of being *created . . . unto good works*. The phrase *which God hath before ordained* shows that God's purpose for believers to do good works was not an afterthought but a forethought that goes all the way back to before the creation of the world. If good works are so important to God, then doing what we can to get ready for good works should become a priority to us. When it does, we will study God's Word faithfully, for it makes us *thoroughly furnished unto all good works*.

7. What would you say to someone who told you that God is happy when we do good works but understands if we don't?

## Work to Prepare for the Judgment Seat of Christ

Good works are the product of salvation, but they do not appear automatically just because we are born again. It is our responsibility to *work out [our] own salvation with fear and trembling* (Phil. 2:12). When we devote ourselves to following God and pleasing Him, good works will follow (2 Cor. 5:9).

8. Read Philippians 2:13. Why should the truths of verse 13 prompt you to do good works?

While we are not born again because of our good works, we will be judged for them. After God snatches the church from the earth at the Rapture, Christians will appear before the Judgment Seat of Christ.

9. Read 2 Corinthians 5:9, 10. What will be the basis for the eternal rewards Christ gives to believers?

We must give account for the use of our lives. Notice the phrase *the things done in his body* (2 Cor. 5:10). Since Christ will reward every good work done for Him out of proper attitudes and motives, we need to strive to accomplish the works He saved us to do. He expects us to have good works to offer Him, and He gives us the Word to equip us for those good works.

James teaches us that we show our faith by our deeds (James 2:20). Without deeds, our faith is proved to be dead. Others observe the reality of our faith in the reality of our works. These works multiply as we spend time in God's Word and become *throughly furnished unto all good works* (2 Tim. 3:17). How much a believer studies the Bible will affect him or her for eternity. Those who grasp this profound truth in this life will be forever grateful they did.

## Work to Imitate Christ

Good works are believers' choices to treat others as Jesus did. The Gospels are full of examples of Jesus' good works. His good works clearly identified Him as the Messiah.

As we abide in Christ, He will do His work through us. *He that believeth on me*, Jesus said, *the works that I do shall he do also; and greater works than these shall he do; because I go unto my Father* (John 14:12). This is a significant statement. Will we really do greater works than Christ?

10. Which one of Christ's works first comes to mind when you read John 14:12?

What did Christ mean when He said we would do greater works than Him? Did He mean we would top His water-walking miracle? He meant that our works are greater than His in quantity, not quality. Multiplied millions have carried out Christ's work.

11. Read John 13:3–17. What type of work was Christ talking about?

God calls us to work to imitate Christ in a foot-washing sort of way, not in a water-walking sort of way.

12. What characterizes the person who voluntarily washes another's dirty feet?

13. What acts of service represent the spirit of foot washing today?

Good works are not about glory and praise but about humbly imitating Christ. Remember that in the last lesson we learned that God created and saved us to bring *Him* glory. Service done for our own praise is not really service at all.

## Prepare your Heart

Actions grow out of character just as surely as apples grow from an apple tree. As we study the Bible, we receive the doctrine, reproof, correction, and instruction in righteousness promised in 2 Timothy 3:16. They shape our character.

Good works are not just an outward conformity to godly actions. They are the reflection of a changed character. As we discussed in lesson nine, the Word of God will examine our motives—the very thoughts and intents of our hearts (Heb. 4:12).

14. Read Hebrews 4:12, 13. What truths in these verses warn us against thinking that our hearts do not matter as long as we do good works outwardly?

After our thoughts and motives are exposed to the light of truth, we will be able to deal with the significant sin problems of our hearts. A changed heart will yield a changed life.

## Share your Heart

Truly Biblical love treats others as God treats them. Good works are acts of love. They carry the love of God into others' lives. As we prepare our hearts with God's Word, we will develop God's love in our hearts. Within our sphere of influence, we can assist our brothers and sisters in Christ to know the Savior more fully by loving them with the Savior's love.

15. Read 1 Thessalonians 4:9. How does God teach believers to love one another?

You can start sharing your love by offering the good works of encouragement and exhortation to others. As relationships build, you can seek out specific needs that you can meet in other believers' lives.

Our church is the key place to share your love. The interconnection of relationships there will allow for many needs to be met through good works.

Good works require sacrifice. Expect to spend time in preparation and follow-up, and do not be surprised if they at times require you to sacrifice financially.

## Effects of Good Works

As we begin to do good works, we will grow in our desire and in our preparation to do more of them. That desire will lead us back to the Word with hunger and enthusiasm. Daily devotions are drudgery unless we are doing them to build ourselves up and prepare to be used by God. If we approach the Bible while seeking specific help in our areas of need, we will have no problem setting the necessary time aside. When we realize that the Bible will allow us to know God and deepen our relationship with Him as it fully equips us to live, we will *desire the sincere milk of the word, that [we] may grow thereby* (1 Pet. 2:2).

If you love the Lord, you are eager for opportunities to share His salvation with others. The Scriptures have shown you that God has met your greatest need, and you find yourself surrounded by others who have that same need, but their need is unmet.

Good works create opportunities for evangelism. For example, Peter exhorted persecuted believers to do good, even if they suffer for their choice (1 Pet. 3:9–14).

16. Read 1 Peter 3:15. Why does suffering for Christ help believers communicate the gospel message to the unsaved?

We are naturally defensive and self-protective, but Peter commands good works in the midst of our suffering. They have an unexpected result. Our willingness not to strike out at those who make life miserable is actually submission to the lordship of Christ and a testimony of our faith. God's Word instructs us, *But sanctify the Lord God in your hearts: and be ready always to give an answer to every man that asketh you a reason of the hope that is in you with meekness and fear* (3:15).

When we submit to Christ's lordship in our trials, people notice. Most people live for themselves. Showing Christ raises interest in our character. We gain the opportunity to share the hope that guides our good works and that keeps us from sinful actions and reactions (Matt. 5:16).

Good works are not a substitute for sharing the gospel verbally. Some Christians wrongly believe that they will never have to risk the embarrassment of verbal witness if they just live good lives.

17. Read Romans 10:13, 14. How important is the believer's verbal witness in winning the unsaved?

Watching someone live for Christ will never get a sinner to Heaven. Since *faith cometh by hearing, and hearing by the word of God* (Rom. 10:17), we must seek opportunities to speak the word of salvation. Good works can create those opportunities—sharing Christ verbally is a good work.

Our Lord Jesus promised His disciples, *I am the vine, ye are the branches: He that abideth in me, and I in him, the same bringeth forth much fruit: for without me ye can do nothing* (John 15:5). We bear fruit when we abide in Him. We abide in Him when we obey Him (15:10). We obey Him when we love others (15:17). As we abide and obey, we bear fruit that remains (15:16). Our closeness to God comes from a heart that loves what He loves and values what He values. This is a lifestyle, not a momentary event.

## MAKING IT PERSONAL

18. Would you say your life is characterized by good works? Explain.

19. What is the connection between your level of good works and your time in God's Word?

20. Why do you do good works?

21. What attitudes or motives might you need to adjust as you carrying out good works?